The Gladstone Pottery Museum, Longton.

Shire County Guide 11

STAFFORDSHIRE

Peter Heaton

Shire Publications Ltd

CONTENTS

Printed in Great Britain by C. I. Thomas & Sons (Haverfordwest) Ltd, Press Buildings, Merlins
Bridge, Haverfordwest, Dyfed SA61 1XF.

British Library Cataloguing in Publication Data: Heaton, Peter. *Staffordshire.* — 2nd ed. —
(Shire County Guide; 11). 1. Staffordshire — visitors' guides. I. Title. 914.24604859. ISBN
0-7478-0113-4.

ACKNOWLEDGEMENTS
The author acknowledges with gratitude the assistance of the following in the preparation of
this book: Ian Cass, Bob Meeson, Lichfield District Council, Stafford Borough Council,
Staffordshire County Council, Staffordshire County Record Office, Staffordshire Moorlands
District Council, Stoke-on-Trent City Council, Tamworth Borough Council, Walsall Borough
Council, Wolverhampton Borough Council.
    Photographs on the following pages are acknowledged to: Tony Boydon Photography, 3, 32,
55; Alfred E. Bristow, 47; Norman Jones (Industrial Photography) Ltd, 28; Cadbury Lamb,
cover, 2, 8, 16, 18, 24, 26 (both), 27, 40, 41, 44, 57; *Leek Post and Times,* 9; Lichfield Tourist
Information Centre, 20, 51; David Peters, 61; Staffordshire County Council, 1, 4; Stoke-on-
Trent City Museums, 22; Josiah Wedgwood and Sons Ltd, 6, 33; David A. Wilkins, 31. The
map on page 63 is by D. R. Darton. The photographs on pages 36, 42, 58 are by the author.

Cover: *Shugborough.*

Below: *Rock houses, Kinver.*

The Tixall Gatehouse, near Shugborough.

1
An undiscovered county

In terms of population, Staffordshire is the fifth biggest of all the shire counties in England and Wales. More than one million people live within its boundaries, which stretch from south Cheshire and the Peak District in the north to border with the county of Hereford and Worcester and the West Midlands conurbation in the south, and from Shropshire in the west across to Derbyshire, Leicestershire and Warwickshire in the east.

Staffordshire is rich in architecture, history and scenery, and there are few counties which are as diverse: diverse in scenic beauty, from the wild crags of the Staffordshire Moorlands to the rolling agricultural landscape of south Staffordshire; diverse in atmosphere, from bustling street markets to villages little changed in hundreds of years; and diverse in its character, from the distinctive dialect of north Staffordshire to the unmistakable Black Country twang found in the south of the county.

Staffordshire has a rich industrial heritage, for it was in the forefront of the industrial revolution, when the technology that provided the industrial base of the county's prosperity developed. The iron and steel industry expanded and thrived in southern Staffordshire and this led to the development of engineering, which remains a major industry both in Staffordshire and throughout the western Midlands.

The ceramic industry in the north of the county is recognised throughout the world as the major centre for the production of quality china and earthenware, a reputation that has been maintained for more than two centuries. The history of the industry is brought to life in museums for visitors and tourists and pottery manufacture is an important contributor to British exports.

The brewing industry centred in Burton upon Trent also grew over the centuries to provide for expanding markets, and coal mining in several areas of Staffordshire grew to meet the demand for energy created by these and other expanding industries.

Traditional industries in Staffordshire have been joined by a variety of new ones, and it is perhaps a measure of the county's industrial success that it is so widely believed that Staffordshire is a largely industrial county.

The Essex Bridge, Great Haywood.

While placenames like Burton upon Trent, Stoke-on-Trent, Lichfield, Cannock, Tamworth, Stafford and Newcastle-under-Lyme are well known, few people outside Staffordshire know the county well. The image of factory chimneys, the Potteries and the Black Country still persists though some four-fifths of Staffordshire is rural and the Black Country towns such as Wolverhampton and Walsall were removed from Staffordshire in the local government reorganisation of 1974. However, many people still regard these towns as belonging to Staffordshire, and because of this and their long historical associations with the county they are included in this book.

The largely rural nature of Staffordshire is most apparent to the rail or motorway traveller looking out of the window while passing through the county, as many thousands of people do each day, since Staffordshire is traversed from north to south by the main railway between London and the north-west of England and the M6 motorway, one of the busiest in Britain.

Yet Staffordshire remains a county undiscovered by outsiders. This is not because its towns and countryside lack charm or its people are unfriendly, but rather because Staffordshire goes quietly about its business without fuss or fanfares.

Thus Staffordshire's successes and attractions are not always readily associated with the county. Much of the spectacular Peak District lies within Staffordshire; Cannock Chase is an officially designated Area of Outstanding Natural Beauty. Alton Towers leisure park is one of Britain's most popular tourist attractions, visited by two million people every year. The University of Keele has an enviable reputation in many fields and internationally renowned companies like Wedgwood, JCB, Ind Coope, Bass, Royal Doulton and Michelin have their bases in Staffordshire.

Agriculture is the county's biggest industry nonetheless, employing more than five thousand people. Much of the farmland is pasture, grass being an important crop upon which the county's large herds of dairy cattle depend. Staffordshire's farmers contribute many colourful events to the county calendar, including the two-day County Show held each summer. Staffordshire College of Agriculture at Rodbaston, managed by the county council, provides residential and day release courses for more than six hundred full and part time students.

Another notable feature of Staffordshire is its canals. It has more than any other county in England, and these, together with the heritage of other industries such as pottery and mining, are an important component of the growing tourist industry. Farm and activity holidays are also increasingly popular, covering pursuits ranging from hang-gliding to cycling. Cycle hire holidays were pioneered in Staffordshire.

Although tourism has grown, Staffordshire was for a long time off the established tourist itineraries and has retained much of its natural charm and atmosphere. It is perhaps because of those increasingly rare qualities that Staffordshire is now at last beginning to be discovered.

Staffordshire's history dates from before the last ice age. The discoveries of two axes have led archaeologists to believe that there were settlements at Shenstone and Drayton Bassett in the south-east of the county around thirty thousand years ago. Flint and bone tools estimated to have been produced around 9000 BC have been discovered in caves in the Manifold valley in north Staffordshire, and tools made after 4500 BC have been discovered in many parts of the county. Several barrows and standing stones can still be found. The Celts had a strong influence over the area from about 600 BC and many hillforts survive throughout the county. The largest is at Castle Ring, which occupies some 9 acres (3.6 ha) at the highest point of Cannock Chase.

In AD 48 the Romans marched into Staffordshire and they established a base at *Letocetum*, now known as Wall, near Lichfield.

The Anglians settled in the county towards the end of the sixth century AD, and their strongholds eventually became part of the kingdom of Mercia, centred on Tamworth. The most famous of the missionaries who worked to convert the Anglians to Christianity was St Chad. His church may have stood on the site of the present-day Lichfield Cathedral.

It was probably during the reign of Edward, son of King Alfred, that the county of Staffordshire was created, centred on his daughter Ethelfreda's fortified settlement at Stafford, from which it took its name. Today Stafford remains the county town.

Three years after the Norman Conquest, William I came to Staffordshire to put down rebels and take over manors. He enlarged forests as royal hunting areas, and the present-day Cannock Chase, for example, 20,000 acres (8100 ha) in extent, is only part of the huge original forest designated by William.

During the middle ages many fine churches were built in Staffordshire (some are described in chapter 5 of this book) but perhaps the most significant development of this time was the rebuilding of Lichfield Cathedral in its distinctive three-spire style.

Industry, though on a small scale, started to spring up, with mines, ironworks, pottery kilns, alabaster workings and glassworks all operating in the county.

Roman Catholicism survived the Reformation in Staffordshire in some strength. Protestant dissent was spreading by the seventeenth century. The last heretic to be burned at the stake in England was executed at Lichfield by the Anglican authorities in 1612. He was a Staffordshire man, Edward Weightman from Burton upon Trent.

In the Civil War Tamworth, Lichfield's Cathedral Close, Tutbury and Stafford were garrisoned by the Royalists. Lichfield held out until 1646, when the central spire of the cathedral was destroyed by a Roundhead bombardment.

The medieval industries of the county continued to develop. The first blast furnace in the Midlands is thought to have been set up by Lord Paget at his ironworks on Cannock Chase in the 1560s. Brewing was developing at Burton at about the same time, and in the

Tutbury Castle.

north of the county Burslem was becoming the capital of the pottery industry.

The industrial revolution brought fame to Staffordshire, led by figures such as Josiah Wedgwood. In 1769 he built a factory in open country west of Hanley, with a house for himself and a village for his workers. The new settlement was named Etruria, and Etruria Hall was restored to form the centrepiece of the National Garden Festival in 1986.

Wedgwood installed steam engines and experimented with new products. Josiah Spode developed bone china at his works in Stoke-on-Trent and Longton grew up on the bone china trade in the nineteenth century.

In the south of the county, John Wilkinson pioneered the use of coal in smelting, revolutionising the area's iron industry, and coalfields were developing to fuel the potteries and the iron furnaces. New mining communities grew up at Hednesford and Chasetown after 1850.

Staffordshire became one of the most densely populated counties in England as a result of the industrial revolution, and the Potteries and the Black Country became important new industrial regions during this period.

Staffordshire County Council was created under the Local Government Act of 1888, which also set up the county boroughs of Hanley, Walsall, West Bromwich and Wolverhampton. Burton upon Trent was awarded the same status in 1901 and Smethwick in 1906. In 1910 the Six Towns of the Potteries federated to form the County Borough of Stoke-on-Trent, which became a city in 1925.

Further changes to the boundaries of Staffordshire came with local government reorganisation in 1974, when much of the southern part of the county was incorporated into the West Midlands Metropolitan County. At the same time Stoke-on-Trent and Burton upon Trent lost their old County Borough status.

Staffordshire's history is carefully preserved by the County Record Office in Stafford. There, the County Archivist is responsible for three repositories, each with a public search room. These are the County Record Office itself, the William Salt Library and the Lichfield Joint Record Office.

Many famous people were born in Staffordshire. They include the actor David Garrick and his friend Dr Samuel Johnson, both of Lichfield, the sculptor Sir Charles Wheeler and the opera singer Dame Maggie Teyte, both from Wolverhampton, and the landscape painter, Peter de Wint, who was born at Stone. The writer Jerome K. Jerome was born at Walsall and Arnold Bennett, the novelist, at Hanley. The author of *The Compleat Angler*, Izaak Walton, came from Stafford. Distinguished industrialists include Josiah Wedgwood, born in Burslem, the 'Iron Man', John Wilkinson, who pioneered the early iron industry, from Wolverhampton, and Sir Charles and John Marston, also of Wolverhampton, who founded Sunbeam Motors and made the famous Villiers engines. Other pioneers of a different kind were Admiral Lord Anson the explorer, born at Shugborough Hall, and John Jervis, Lord St Vincent, from Stone, both great sailors of their time.

Other well known figures with Staffordshire associations are Captain Smith, master of the ill fated *Titanic*, who is commemorated by a statue in Beacon Park, Lichfield, and Sir Robert Peel, the nineteenth-century prime minister, who was Member of Parliament for Tamworth for many years.

The statue of Josiah Wedgwood at Barlaston.

Cannock Chase.

2
Staffordshire's countryside

'England can show nothing more beautiful and nothing more ugly than the works of nature and the works of man within the limits of the county': so wrote Arnold Bennett when the industrial revolution in Staffordshire was at its height. Today Staffordshire remains beautiful, but its industrial legacy is being turned to advantage as an attraction for tourists.

PEAK DISTRICT NATIONAL PARK

The upland country of north Staffordshire is particularly impressive. On the windy ridges of the Staffordshire Moorlands, a few miles north of Leek, on the edge of the Peak District National Park, stand the Roaches (from the French *roche*, a rock), a tor-like outcrop of rocks. From their summit on a fine day Cheshire can be seen stretching flat as a table-top across to Wales. Nearby, Flash, at 1518 feet (463 metres), is the highest village in England, near the point where Staffordshire, Cheshire and Derbyshire meet.

To the east of Leek lie the beautiful valleys of the rivers Hamps, Manifold and Dove, which are a part of the Peak District national park. Since Izaak Walton, author of *The Compleat Angler*, and his friend Charles Cotton first cast their lines around the village of Ilam, these waters have tempted anglers after trout, and the scenery has drawn many others in search of relaxation.

Much of this area of the 'White Peak' is carved out of massive beds of limestone and it is impossible to walk far along these valleys without finding evidence of it. In places the streams disappear underground entirely during the summer and everywhere running water has hollowed out ravines and potholes and formed waterfalls. Near Wetton the hillside has been hollowed out to produce the spectacular Thor's Cavern. Here, and at Ossoms Cave and Thor's Fissure in the Manifold valley, archaeologists have discovered traces of stone age man.

The hidden valleys of north Staffordshire are as memorable as the high moors and include the romantic wooded slopes of the Churnet valley, sometimes known as the English Rhineland, and picturesque Dovedale. Activity holidays in Britain were pioneered

Izaak Walton's Cottage, Shallowford.

in north Staffordshire and today orienteering, bicycle hire holidays, pony trekking, bird watching, plant study, industrial archaeology and canals are some of the themes available to the holidaymaker who wants something a little out of the ordinary.

More traditionally, long-distance footpaths like the Staffordshire Way, the Tissington Trail and the High Peak Trail provide other means of exploring the countryside away from the car. Details of these are available from tourist information offices or from the county council's Planning and Development Officer. Forest parks and country parks throughout the county mean that easy access to the countryside is never far away.

CANNOCK CHASE

In mid Staffordshire lies Cannock Chase, over 20,000 acres (8100 ha) of magnificent heath and woodland scenery, accessible at many points, yet remote and secluded in parts. Cannock Chase is an Area of Outstanding Natural Beauty, as well as one of the largest country parks in Britain, and yet over three million people live within 20 miles (32 km) of it. The Chase provides for leisurely picnics and walks as well as for more strenuous activities like orienteering and long-distance walking on the Staffordshire Way. There are also opportunities for field studies not only of plant and animal life, but also of the develop-

ment of man's activities in the area. In the heart of the Chase is the Marquis Drive Visitor Centre and the Forestry Commission centre, which tell the story of the area and its wildlife.

In Norman times Cannock Forest was a hunting ground for royalty and hunting lodges were built at Cannock Wood. Later the Bishops of Lichfield acquired Cannock Chase, as it has become known, and continued to hunt deer and boar in its extensive oakwoods. Deer roam freely across the Chase, as they have done for nearly a thousand years. The fallow deer are thought to have been introduced by the Bishops of Lichfield and there are now several hundred of them. The Chase is one of the best places in England to observe fallow deer in their natural surroundings. Red deer can be seen also, but in smaller numbers. Fallow deer are most likely to be seen either early in the morning or an hour or so before dusk. The Sherbrook valley is a particularly good area for sightings. Those motoring across the Chase should remember, however, that deer may be on the move throughout the day, and many are killed or injured by thoughtless drivers.

Cannock Chase dominates Staffordshire's central belt, providing recreation and rural tranquillity for thousands of visitors from throughout the western Midlands. It is countryside with a rich and varied character, from wild rolling heathland to secluded valleys and sheltered woodland. Between the great Forestry Commission plantations which clothe much of the area lie the softer features of oak and birch woodland, heather and gorse richly coloured in the summer and the green carpets of bracken and Cannock Chase berry, a type of bilberry.

From the heights of Castle Ring (see chapter 3) and Brereton Spurs there are extensive views over the valley of the river Trent and from vantage points north of Brindley Heath, towards Brocton, the hills of Shropshire and the Welsh borders can clearly be seen.

In a small valley near Broadhurst Green 6 acres (2.4 ha) of land form a German military cemetery. This unique place stands as a memorial to some five thousand German war dead, mostly soldiers, but also including some Kriegsmarine and Luftwaffe men. The Ger-

Dry stone walling being demonstrated near Leek.

man graves have headstones of Belgian granite and are set in plots of heather. They are tended by the English gardeners of the Commonwealth War Graves Commission. The first moves towards establishing the cemetery were made in 1959 by the Germans, who looked at the possibility of a site next to the Commonwealth War Cemetery on the Chase. This cemetery contains 388 graves from the two world wars, of which 287 are of German servicemen. The people of Staffordshire, through the county council, gave the land to the Commonwealth War Graves Commission for the creation of a German cemetery, and German servicemen from both wars — sailors buried at seaports around the coast of Britain, airmen shot down inland and soldiers, mostly prisoners of war, buried in numerous country churchyards, were transferred from their places of burial to plots in the cemetery between 1964 and 1966. German servicemen who were buried in British military cemeteries and in war grave plots in civilian cemeteries were not moved. Today many thousands of visitors see the cemeteries on Cannock Chase, whether they are simply out for the day or on the tourist round, or are relatives or friends of those who have a place in the cemeteries. Frequently there are flowers or wreaths laid by, or on behalf of, people for whom the cemetery has special meaning. Anyone who stops and looks around there cannot fail to be moved by the surroundings.

The Chase has other associations with the First World War. It was the last billet for thousands of the young men who were being trained to fight in France. Today the many reminders of that period have been linked into a Great War Trail by the county council's Planning Department.

Many footpaths cross the Chase and at Marquis Drive, Brindley Heath, Whitehouse and other places car parks and picnic areas provide good bases for exploring the area. Trail guides have been produced and forest walks marked out, details of which can be obtained from the visitor centre at Marquis Drive or from the Forestry Commission's Forest Centre at Birches Valley, which also features a most interesting deer museum.

On the southern boundaries of Cannock Chase are the 300 acres (120 ha) of the Hednesford Hills, much of which is a registered common. The hills are criss-crossed by many paths, some used in the past by miners on their way to work at local collieries,

Froghall quarries. The site of the old wharf is now a picnic area.

others by racehorses trained at Hednesford and Rawnsley. A walk around Hednesford Hills gives good views across Cannock Chase and the communities around it. To the west is Hednesford Park, where there was once a pool said to have been abounding with pike, perch and roach.

To the west of Cannock lies Shoal Hill Common, 180 acres (73 ha) of heathland and oak and birch woodland, and a delightful spot for a picnic within easy reach of the centre of Cannock.

THE VALE OF TRENT

Between the Peak District National Park and Tamworth in the south of Staffordshire is an unheralded but delightful piece of countryside, drained by the river Trent and its tributaries. Isolated by dense forest and seasonal flooding, the vale and many of its smaller communities used to have only tenuous communications with the outside world. Today, although easily accessible, the area remains largely unspoiled and rich in local traditions.

At the heart of the Vale of Trent are ancient villages such as Newborough and Abbots Bromley, where ceremonies commemo-rating the life of the old hunting forests which once dominated the area are still held. The historic city of Lichfield is also surrounded by attractive countryside.

SOUTH STAFFORDSHIRE

In the district of South Staffordshire, there are large designated Special Landscape Areas. Probably the most notable is Kinver Edge, in the southernmost part of the county, where Staffordshire borders the county of Hereford and Worcester. Kinver Edge is now in the care of the National Trust, while Kinver itself is described in the Domesday Book.

COUNTRY PARKS, PICNIC AREAS, COUNTRY TRAILS ETC

Staffordshire County Council, through its County Planning and Development Officer, provides and manages some 5000 acres (2020 ha) of country parks and picnic areas throughout the county. The Lichfield estate donated around 2000 acres (800 ha) of Cannock Chase to the county council in 1957, and the holding has now been enlarged to form one of the largest country parks in Britain. In addition, there are several beautiful country parks and picnic sites in other attractive parts of the county. The county council's Countryside Division runs an excellent programme of guided walks throughout Staffordshire.

Brereton Spurs Picnic Site (OS 128: SK 055155).
A part of Cannock Chase, Brereton Spurs comprise nearly 90 acres (36 ha) of heathland and provide dramatic views over the Trent valley, near Rugeley.

Cannock Chase Country Park: Marquis Drive Visitor Centre (OS 127: SJ 990175).
The sights and sounds of the history and the wildlife of the Chase are part of the visitor's introduction to the Chase at the visitor centre. The views are superb and there is information about nature trails to follow. There is also the Great War Trail which covers an area used as a military training ground for soldiers and visits Commonwealth and German military cemeteries and the Polish Katyn Memorial (see also above).

Cannock Forest Centre (OS 128: SK 018170).
The Deer and Forest Museum is here (see also above).

Churnet Valley Picnic Place (OS 119: SK 053457)
At Oakamoor on the B5417 3 miles (5 km) east of Cheadle is a grassy area of 15 acres (6 ha) on what was once an industrial site.

Consall Nature Park
Roughly a mile (1.6 km) south-east of Wetley Rocks, on minor roads from the A520 and A522, a series of steep, wooded valleys to the west of the river Churnet provide not only a wild and spectacular landscape but also an area of great wildlife interest. There are also remains of old ironstone workings.

Coombes Valley (OS 118: SJ 996514).
Off B5063 south-east of Leek, a 261 acre (105 ha) reserve owned by the Royal Society for the Protection of Birds is a refuge for woodland birds. For information contact RSPB Reserves Division, telephone: 0767 80551.

Deep Hayes Country Park (OS 118: SJ 960532).
On minor roads off the A53 near Longsdon, about 3 miles (5 km) south-west of Leek, Deep Hayes Country Park is centred around an old canal feeder reservoir now refashioned into three smaller pools. The whole area is a delight to walk through and a series of flower-filled meadows, small marshes and scrub woodlands provides wildlife interest. There are magnificent views of the north Staffordshire countryside, and a visitor centre.

Froghall Wharf (OS 119 or 128: SK 022477).
Off the A52 and B5417 3 miles (5 km) north of Cheadle, this picnic site of about 8 acres (3.2 ha) is centred on the terminus of the Caldon Canal. The site includes a former canal warehouse, now restored as a restaurant, with a small shop and a base for horse-drawn canal-boat trips with guides to tell visitors the history of the canal (see chapter 9).

Greenway Bank Country Park (OS 118: SJ 889552). Telephone: 0782 518200.
1 mile (1.6 km) south of Biddulph, off the A527, there are 110 acres (45 ha) of woodlands and lakes of a nineteenth-century landscaped estate, including Knypersley Pool, with a visitor centre.

Hanbury Common Picnic Site (OS 128: SK 174258).
Just west of Tutbury, between Uttoxeter and Burton upon Trent, this is a small area of brambles and trees with beautiful views over the Dove valley.

Hanchurch Hills (OS 127: SJ 839397).
South-west of Hanchurch, off the A519, near its junction with the A5182, is this area of secluded walks and picnic spots, with 19 acres (7.6 ha) of open woodland, within easy reach of Stoke-on-Trent.

Hanley Forest Park
This forest park, located within the centre of Hanley, aims to recreate a rural environment close to a city centre and is managed by the Stoke-on-Trent City Council. There are facilities for formal and informal recreation.

Highgate Common Country Park (OS 138: SO 838896).
3 miles (5 km) south-west of Wombourne, between Wombourne and Kinver, Highgate Common comprises nearly 300 acres (120 ha) of open heath and woodland, with a wide variety of bird life.

Ilam Park, Ilam (OS 119: SK 131507).
Off the A515, north-west of Ashbourne, the 84 acres (34 ha) of park and woods lie on both sides of the river Manifold. There is an information centre with a shop and a tearoom.

Kinver Edge (OS 138: SO 835830).
This beautiful wood- and heath-covered sandstone ridge owned by the National Trust also has cave dwellings at Holy Austin Rock which were inhabited until the 1960s (see under Kinver in chapter 10).

Mow Cop (OS 118: SJ 857574).
Mow Cop is a folly built in 1754 on a high rocky outcrop on the Staffordshire and Cheshire border 2 miles (3 km) north of Kidsgrove. 1100 feet (335 metres) above sea level, it is a superb vantage point for views across the surrounding countryside. Mow Cop is a place of pilgrimage for Methodists, for at its summit in 1819 Hugh Bourne, a local carpenter and builder, held meetings and out of these, condemned by the Wesleyan Methodist Conference, Primitive Methodism was born.

Park Hall Country Park , Weston Coyney, Stoke-on-Trent (OS 118: SJ 936446). Telephone: 0782 331889.
333 acres (135 ha) of heath and conifer woodland here have been reclaimed from former sand and gravel quarries. There are views over the Potteries and east to the Pennines, and canyon-like quarries have been retained for picnic sites.

Rudyard Lake (OS 118: SJ 951583).
4 miles (6 km) north-west of Leek on the A523 is Rudyard Lake. 2 miles (3 km) long, it was built in 1797 as a reservoir for the Caldon Canal. The lake, from which Rudyard Kipling was named, has steep, wooded banks and pleasant walks and picnic areas. There are also sailing, fishing and birdwatching.

Stafford Doxey Marshes Nature Reserve (OS 127: SJ 908243)
About 1 mile (1.6 km) north-west of the town, this reserve attracts a variety of birds, which can be watched from a hide.

The Staffordshire Way
This fine long-distance footpath, accessible by bus and rail, passes through some of the county's finest scenery. The route measures 93 miles (150 km), starting in the north on the gritstone edge of Mow Cop, with wide views over the Cheshire Plain to the Welsh mountains, and then passing through the secret valley of the Churnet, along the Dove Valley, and over the scarplands of the Needwood Forest to the heart of Cannock Chase. From here the way runs over the rolling hills of south-west Staffordshire before reaching the sandstone outcrops of Kinver Edge. Most people tackle the route in sections. It is well signed and there are interesting circular walks from the main route. Guide books are available from Staffordshire County Council's Planning Department.

Tittesworth Reservoir (OS 118: SJ 994604)
3 miles (5 km) north-east of Leek, reached by minor roads off the A53, Tittesworth Reservoir was created in 1875 by the Potteries Waterworks Company to provide a water supply for mill owners when the spring water they had been using was taken by the company. The lake looks entirely natural and beautifully mirrors the moors all around it. There is a picnic area and fishing.

Walsall Arboretum
Parks of the traditional kind abound throughout Staffordshire and Wolverhampton in particular has many fine examples, but perhaps the finest is Walsall Arboretum, 79 acres (32 ha) of parkland close to the town centre, yet giving the visitor the feeling of being in the heart of the countryside. The focal point of the arboretum is its fine lake, originally a disused limestone quarry. Now there are fishing, wild ducks, waterfowl and boating, and a miniature steam railway runs nearby at weekends during the summer.
Each September the arboretum is the home of the Walsall Illuminations, which attract more than a quarter of a million visitors to the town each year.

3
Archaeological sites

It has been said that Staffordshire yields its secrets slowly and this is certainly true of its archaeology. Bronze age burials, Roman camps and medieval villages lie hidden below the ground. Nevertheless there is still much for the visitor to see, and some of this is outlined in the following section. Many of the visitors who come to Staffordshire enter the county on one of the two major Roman roads, these being Watling Street (now the A5) and Ryknild Street (today's A38).

The Manifold valley

Ancient earthworks have survived unusually well in the area of the Manifold valley in north Staffordshire. Bronze age burial mounds and ancient earthworks lie in a valley landscape of medieval cultivation terraces and field systems scattered with deserted villages, a ruined hall, a deer park, a priory grange, an eighteenth-century house, limestone farmhouses and limekilns, and overlain by a web of dry stone walls. It is an archaeological heritage of outstanding national significance, accessible to the general public through public rights of way.

Examples of barrows are those at Ilam Tops Low (grid reference SK 136527), north of Castern Hall (SK 126529), south of Stanshope (SK 128539) and Mere Hill (SK 105526).

Prehistoric settlement is indicated by a flint-working site near Throwley Cottage (SK 108519) and prehistoric, Roman and Anglo-Saxon finds have been made in a number of caves.

The medieval nucleated hamlet of Castern (SK 123525) has now shrunk to a hall and a farm while Throwley, deserted between about 1377 and 1524, is now a single farm. At Musden (SK 123512) was a medieval grange to Croxden Abbey on land mentioned in the original endowment of 1176: the terraced hillside site of the grange is still a significant landscape feature. At the edge of Throwley is the striking limestone ruin of Throwley Old Hall, a medieval hall and cross-wing adapted into a Tudor country house.

Medieval settlement of the area had an enormous and beneficial impact on the landscape. Medieval and post-medieval ridge and furrow and impressive strip lynchets survive in abundance. These sinuous long ridges, hollows and terraces reflect a former arable farming practice which was systematically repeated for generations. Whereas elsewhere in Staffordshire (and England as a whole) much ridge and furrow has been obliterated, subsequent pastoral use of the land has ensured its survival in the Manifold valley, where it forms a significant element of the landscape. Traces of former boundaries of long narrow fields can also be seen north-west of Throwley Hall (SK 116517) and north-west of Castern (SK 120528). Ancient woodland, probably partially managed from the medieval period, punctuates the field pattern, particularly on steeper slopes near the valley bottom.

A further phase of changing land use can be seen south of Throwley Hall where a stone deer park boundary wall (SK 113521) marks one stage in the decline of arable farming. Later again, and in marked contrast with the earthworks of medieval open field systems are small sub-rectangular fields dating from the seventeenth and eighteenth centuries, enclosed by dry stone walls which form an irregular grid pattern over the earlier landscape. Post-medieval ridge and furrow also survives. It is narrower and straighter than the medieval ridge and furrow and is contained within individual stone-walled fields, often on lower ground. Isolated small quarries, limekilns and stone field barns also occur. Examples of these are north of Castern (SK 119533) and SK 107520), near Ilam Tops (SK 137527), east of Damsgate (SK 133535) and south of Longcote Barn (SK 111514).

NEOLITHIC
The Bridestones burial chamber (SJ 906622).

This ancient burial chamber lies on a minor road off the A523 from Leek, about 2 miles (3 km) north-west of Rudyard Lake. The remains are much smaller than its original size. The cairn was once about 300 feet (91 metres) long and 40 feet (12 metres) wide but in the eighteenth century the mound and two smaller lateral chambers were removed. The surviving parallel-sided burial chamber is 16 feet (4.9 metres) long and is divided into two sections by a broken 'porthole' stone. East of the chamber a forecourt is partly outlined by large stones.

BRONZE AGE
Elford Low, Elfordlowe Farm, Elford, Tamworth (SK 194092).

This bronze age barrow is just south of the village of Elford, on private land, but viewable from the road, since it is immediately against the hedge. Known to local people as Robin Hood's Butts, it contains a prehistoric burial and survives today as a substantial circular mound. From this spot there are good views of the valley of the river Tame and of Hopwas Woods, an outlier of the once vast royal hunting forest of Cannock.

IRON AGE
Castle Ring hillfort, Cannock Chase (SJ 045128).

On the highest point of Cannock Chase, at Cannock Wood, is a fine example of an iron age hillfort. Encompassing 9 acres (3.6 ha), Castle Ring would once have been a centre of activity for the surrounding area. It has three defensive banks and ditches on its east side and one larger bank and ditch on its steeper north side. Today the visitor can stroll round its impressive ramparts, enjoying superb views over the Trent valley.

Kinver promontory fort (SO 836832).

Here there is an iron age promontory fort, defended on the south-west and east by a massive bank and ditch. The bank rises above the interior and falls about 17 feet (5.2 metres) to a ditch. There are fine views from the escarpment on which the fort is built, across the village of Kinver and its valley. The site is in the care of the National Trust.

ROMAN PERIOD
Letocetum, Wall, near Lichfield (SK 099066).

A Roman fort was built here in a hilltop enclosure set across the line of Watling Street, and the place later became a posting station. Much of the business of Imperial Rome was conducted through official couriers who travelled the comprehensive road network, and posting stations were built at intervals for them. The remains of a small Roman settlement can also be seen. To the south, evidence of metalworking was found and there were buildings of the Claudian period which included a granary within the enclosure. A group of Roman buildings west of the forts at Wall included a well preserved bath suite. There is also the site of a cemetery containing burials of the first and second centuries AD. A small museum houses some of the objects which have been found at the site.

Rocester (SK 111038).

Bronze age copper and bronze objects and Roman coins and pottery have been among the many finds at Rocester, where there were Roman buildings within a fortified settlement. There is clear evidence that there were siegeworks, defences and a cemetery there. The military occupation is thought to have ceased between 120 and 150 AD, to be succeeded by later Roman and post-Roman civilian settlement.

MEDIEVAL PERIOD
Wychnor deserted village (SK 177161).

At Wychnor, north of Alrewas and west of the A38, is perhaps the finest deserted medieval village in Staffordshire. An extensive area of impressive earthworks is visible from the lanes and from a public footpath which crosses the site. At the heart of the former village, the church of St Lawrence has masonry which displays its Norman origins.

The deserted village at Stafford Castle is described in chapter 4 under the description of the castle.

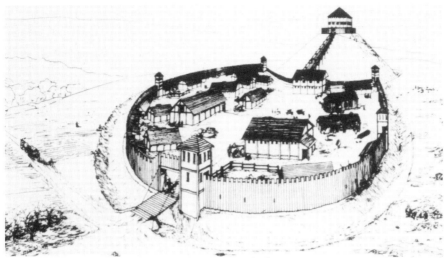

Stafford Castle as it would have appeared when first built.

4
Castles

Chartley Castle, Chartley Holme, on the A515 Stafford-Uttoxeter road.

This is a ruined medieval castle with origins in the eleventh century. On top of a natural hill are a Norman motte and two baileys. In the thirteenth century the motte and inner bailey were converted into a stone castle with a shell keep on the motte, and the bailey was strengthened by a curtain wall with semi-drum towers. In 1153 Chartley Castle passed from the Earl of Chester to the Ferrers family.

Extensive earthworks can be seen around the castle remains, including two moated sites, and an earth dam. The enclosure is quadrangular with the remains of the keep at one end of the motte. At the lower end are two massive circular towers with walls about 12 feet (3.7 metres) thick and with split openings. Mary, Queen of Scots, was a prisoner here from January to September 1586.

Stafford Castle, Newport Road (A518), Stafford. Telephone: 0785 40204 or 57698.

Lying in pleasant countryside a mile or so outside the county town, Stafford Castle is a very well preserved and extensive example of an early Norman earth and timber fortress, with a deserted medieval village site adjacent. In 1348 a stone keep was constructed on the Norman mound. Although partially demolished in the Civil War, it was rebuilt in the Gothic Revival style in about 1800. A castle trail has been marked out for the visitor.

Stafford Castle originated as a massive Norman motte and bailey castle. Built upon a natural ridge, the castle comprised an immense artificial earth mound (the motte) and two large attached enclosures (baileys). The motte and the baileys were defended by impressive surrounding banks and ditches. A timber tower would have been built on the motte, while the baileys would have contained many timber buildings for everyday living, such as halls, kitchens, barns and accommodation.

A castle was first built at Stafford in 1070 following a rebellion in the county against William the Conqueror. It is not clear whether this castle was built by the king inside the walls of the existing Saxon town or on a different site. However, the Domesday Book recorded that 'a castle on Stafford land' had been destroyed. The earliest reference to the new castle is dated 1102, although the land which includes the castle had been granted in 1070 to Robert Toeni of Normandy, who later styled himself Robert de Stafford. In 1348 the first Earl of Stafford commissioned the building of a large and unique stone keep on the Norman mound and, although partially demolished in the Civil War, this was rebuilt in the Gothic Revival style in about 1800. The castle was lived in until 1950, after which it was left to deteriorate, but Stafford Borough Council is now encouraging restoration and archaeological excavation work.

The deserted medieval village came to light as a result of fieldwork in 1978. The earthworks comprise three hollow ways, or sunken roadways, with platforms and terraces probably representing the sites of houses. The hollow ways are roughly parallel and equidistant, suggesting a deliberate grid pattern. The village could have been the Monetvile mentioned in the Domesday Book of 1086. This is a Norman French name meaning the vill near the mountain. The village appears to have been deserted during the fifteenth century. The below-ground remains of the village are among the best preserved of their kind in Britain.

Tamworth Castle Museum, Tamworth. Telephone: 0827 311222 and 63563. A visitor and interpretation centre opens in 1991.

Situated in the centre of the town, Tamworth Castle has one of Britain's largest and best remaining Norman shell keeps. A

Norman motte and bailey castle was built at Tamworth shortly after the Norman Conquest. It is thought that Robert de Despencer was its first lord and responsible for building the mound. He fell into disfavour towards the end of his life, his lands being confiscated and handed over to his nephew-in-law, Roger de Marmion. The Marmions then held Tamworth Castle for several generations as Royal Champions of the Kings of England. The Marmions are thought to have been responsible for the construction of the surviving keep and tower and the curtain wall of herringbone masonry in the twelfth century.

Because it has been inhabited almost continually, the castle displays architecture of many different styles and periods. Within its walls there is a fine late medieval open hall with a massively framed timber roof, and Jacobean state apartments containing an important heraldic frieze and contemporary woodwork.

Notable visitors to the castle have included Edward II in 1325 and James I in 1619, 1621 and 1624, accompanied by Prince Charles (later Charles I) on his second visit.

The castle was held by Royalists in the Civil War and captured in 1643 after two days of siege by Cromwellian forces. In the following year the castle passed through different

Tamworth Castle gardens.

families and it was largely neglected during the first half of the eighteenth century. However, extensive repairs were carried out from 1751 when the castle was acquired by the Townshends.

Tamworth Corporation purchased the castle in 1897 to commemorate the Diamond Jubilee of Queen Victoria. It was formally opened two years later and its fabric and contents provide a fine insight into life in bygone centuries.

The castle also houses a museum which illustrates many aspects of local history. Its contents include sections of the unique Saxon mill which was discovered near Bolebridge in 1971 and a fine collection of Saxon and Norman pennies, which emphasise the importance of the mint at Tamworth during the tenth and eleventh centuries.

Outside the castle, archaeological excavations on the site of a seventeenth-century building which stood between the Castle Gardens and Market Street revealed remains of the original thirteenth-century gatehouse tower as well as the fourteenth-century bridge over the castle moat. This work is of such a high standard that it is believed to have been carried out by royal masons for the Marmion family. The area surrounding the remains has been landscaped.

Tutbury Castle and Country Park, Tutbury, near Burton upon Trent. Telephone: 0283 812129.

A Norman castle was built at Tutbury by Hendry de Ferrers, to whom William the Conqueror gave considerable estates. There had been some previous fortification on the site and iron age and Roman finds have led to speculation that it was built on an ancient occupation site. The Norman castle was one of the motte and bailey type, with a mound (still existing in the south-west corner) protected by a wooden palisade. In 1174 the town and castle were destroyed by the king's forces. A later owner, Robert Ferrers, rebelled against Henry III in 1266 and the king gave the Ferrers estates to his own son, Edmund, who was made Earl of Lancaster in 1267. The castle and the neighbouring estate descended through the earldom of Lancaster, and since 1399 (when Henry Bolingbroke, Duke of Lancaster, came to the throne as Henry IV) they have belonged to the sovereign as part of the Duchy of Lancaster.

The castle had been damaged in the Bar-

ons' War. Edmund and his son Thomas restored and enlarged it, building in 1313-14 the gatehouse popularly attributed to John of Gaunt. John did carry out repairs and improvements, as did his son Henry IV, and both visited Tutbury. The works were continued throughout the fifteenth century, but the castle had already lost its strategic importance and from then on fell into decay.

Mary, Queen of Scots, was imprisoned in Tutbury Castle in 1569-70 and 1585, and James I and Charles I stayed at the castle more than once. In the Civil War it was besieged and fell to the Parliamentarians in April 1646. In the next year the castle was dismantled and largely destroyed. For about one hundred years from the early nineteenth century the castle was occupied as a farm.

Most buildings now standing date from 1400 to 1450, but the house at the south end is less than three hundred years old. The round tower on the motte at the south-west corner is a fake ruin put up towards the end of the eighteenth century on the site of the original keep.

The main parts of the medieval castle that are still visible are the foundations of the chapel, John of Gaunt's Gateway, the High Tower and the south-east range. The foundations of the chapel, in the centre of the interior, date from the late twelfth century and consist of nave and chancel. The main gate at the north end, known as John of Gaunt's Gateway, consists of an early fourteenth-century gatehouse and a barbican of about 1400. The High Tower in the middle of the east side is a four-storey building. A staircase leads to a turret, from which a fine view can be had. The range in the south-east corner is the most extensive part of the ruins. It contains two chambers with fine fireplaces on the upper floor, and two chambers below. The small gateway by which visitors enter the castle yard is a seventeenth-century addition.

Between the south-east range and the custodian's house is the site of a large timbered hall built in the early seventeenth century against the outer wall, which was pierced by rectangular windows. The medieval hall stood a short distance away from this wall. The present house was reconstructed in the seventeenth or eighteenth century. In front of it is a medieval well, 120 feet (37 metres) deep. There are spectacular views of the Dove valley from the castle and country walks in the park.

Croxden Abbey.

5
Churches and religious buildings

Staffordshire has a wealth of fine churches, and this chapter takes a brief look at a few of those which have features or history of particular interest. Some other churches are mentioned under their town or village in chapter 10.

Brereton: St Michael

The most important building in Brereton, near Rugeley, is St Michael's church, which was designed by Thomas Trubshaw in 1837 and forty years later enlarged and improved with a chancel and transepts by Sir George Gilbert Scott. The uppermost part of the church's tower and the spire were added ten years after this by John Aldrid Scott, and in the same year a frieze of vine trails and angels was painted in the nave.

Burton upon Trent: St Modwen

The Irish princess St Modwen built a chapel in the ninth century on an island in the middle of the river Trent at Burton. The parish church dedicated to her was built in 1726. The church is one of the best examples of Palladian-type Gothic architecture in Britain. The church contains a coffer and font dating from 1662 and other relics of earlier times.

There is also a complete set of parish records from 1538.

Cannock: St Luke

The parish church of St Luke is in the centre of Cannock, surrounded by well maintained lawns. According to records, as early as 1143 the church had a chantry and a grammar school linked to it. The battlemented church tower dates from the fourteenth century and it and the west end of the nave are the oldest surviving parts of the building. Displayed there are the arms of Humphrey de Stafford, who was killed at the Battle of Northampton in 1460. The church was extended in the late nineteenth century by two bays, and a new chancel with combined vestry and organ chamber was built. In 1949 the main porch was rebuilt and a war memorial chapel added.

Cheadle: churches of St Giles

Cheadle's two main churches both occupy prominent positions in the town, with the parish church of St Giles and the Catholic church of St Giles both having features of note. The parish church is sited just north of the spot where a medieval church stood (in

18

what is now the cemetery) until 1838, when it was destroyed and the present church built. Some carved stone corbels and some altar rails dated 1687 survive from the old church. The county council's Historic Buildings Record describes the church, with its solid perpendicular tower, as 'a decent Gothic preaching house with a very short chancel and lofty arcades'.

A very striking landmark, with its 200 foot (61 metre) spire, is the Catholic church of St Giles, a Gothic masterpiece of Pugin. This richly decorated church was built at the expense of Lord Shrewsbury in 1846.

Clifton Campville: St Andrew

St Andrew's at Clifton Campville, northeast of Tamworth, has been described as one of the greatest parish churches in England. It is a very beautiful church and its spire is a landmark for miles around. It dates from the thirteenth century, and to this period belong the north transept and the north wall of the nave. The rest is mainly of the mid fourteenth century. The tower has a spire and flying buttresses, with a vaulted ground stage lit by large windows on the north, south and west. The transept is vaulted, with a room above containing a fireplace and garderobe. The nave roof is fourteenth-century while the south chapel and aisle have low-pitched sixteenth-century roofs. There is an alabaster table tomb to Sir John Vernon (1545) with effigies of a knight and lady. Almost every aspect of the church's architecture, furnishings and monuments has attracted widespread praise.

Croxden Abbey (OS 128: SK 065397). 3 miles (5 km) north-west of Uttoxeter off A50. English Heritage.

Of the ruined structure of the medieval abbey founded in 1176, the south wall of the south transept, the west wall of the nave and the east range of the cloisters still stand. There was a choir of the chevet type (an apse, ambulatory and radiating chapels). Vaulting shafts of the south walls show that a rib vault existed. Corbels in the cloisters indicate that at least three bays outside the chapter house were vaulted, or were intended to be vaulted. The eastern range of the abbey was completed after the church. Next to the south transept is a chamber of three bays, two of which formed the sacristy. The last part of the claustral buildings to be completed was the

western range, around 1288-90. The north end was vaulted, with a row of columns in the centre.

Considerable portions of the abbey precinct wall, completed about 1284, still remain and the site of a medieval infirmary dated between 1242 and 1268 is today cut in two by a public road.

Gnosall: St Lawrence

The church probably stands on the site of an Anglo-Saxon church and a secular college. Historically, archaeologically and aesthetically it is one of the most significant churches in the county and was one of the six collegiate churches of Staffordshire. The core of the church is twelfth-century, including the crossing arches and much of the walling. There was refashioning in the thirteenth and fourteenth centuries and the fine fourteenth-century east window has good painted glass dating from 1922. There is a mutilated fifteenth-century effigy of a knight. The north aisle roof is sixteenth-century, but the other roofs are modern.

Hednesford: Our Lady of Lourdes

This unusual Roman Catholic church was erected between 1927 and 1933 as a result of a world-wide appeal for funds by Father P. J. Boyle. The building is strikingly ambitious in its design, to a curious thirteenth-century French style, with its low side chapels, polygonal apse and turret in the corner of one of the transepts. The sculptured stations of the cross are very good examples.

Ilam: St Bertram

The church of the Holy Cross, otherwise St Bertram, in Ilam, is an early medieval church, dating from the twelfth century. It has an unusual saddleback tower. The south chapel is fifteenth-century although it was partly rebuilt in 1618. The font is thought to date from the eleventh century and the base of St Bertram's shrine from the late thirteenth century. There is a large alabaster table tomb to Robert Meverell (1626) and an imposing monument to D. P. Watts (1806). The church was extensively restored in 1856 by Sir George Gilbert Scott. There are two late Anglo-Saxon crosses in the churchyard.

Leek: St Edward the Confessor

The parish church, built in 1297, stands on what is thought to have been the site of a wooden church in Saxon times. There remain some Saxon stones in the churchyard, one of which was a preaching cross more than 10 feet (3 metres) high in its days of use. The church itself has an early sixteenth-century nave, a south porch of 1670, memorials from the sixteenth century and a huge eighteenth-century gallery at the west end of the nave. Fine nineteenth-century features include pulpit and stalls by Street and glass by Morris, among a wealth of Victorian glass.

Lichfield Cathedral: the Blessed Virgin Mary and St Chad

Lichfield Cathedral is famous the world over and unforgettable to those who have visited it. It was begun in 1195 and completed around 1325. It is unusual in having three spires, known throughout the area as the 'Ladies of the Vale'.

The first church was built at Lichfield in 669 and as early as 700 it was the site of the cathedral of Mercia. Visible traces of that period have long since gone and so have those of the Norman cathedral which succeeded it. The present-day Lichfield Cathedral dates largely from the thirteenth and fourteenth centuries and has a colourful history. The Cathedral Close was once enclosed by fortifications and was the scene of violent struggles for power. During the Civil War the cathedral was fortified by the Royalists and captured twice by the Parliamentarians. Signs of battle show today in the fabric of the buildings despite the efforts of restoration. Cannonballs have been unearthed in neighbouring gardens.

The interior of the cathedral measures 370 feet (113 metres) from end to end. Some of its many treasures are the sixteenth-century Herckenrode glass from Liège in Belgium, in the Lady Chapel, Sir Francis Chantry's statue of the Sleeping Children and the eighth-century Gospels of St Chad. There are also busts of two of Lichfield's notable figures, David Garrick and Samuel Johnson, both dating from 1793.

The earliest surviving portion of the cathedral is the three west bays of the chancel, which date from around 1200. The nave was built in the late thirteenth century. The magnificent crossing is further enhanced by a brass and iron Victorian pulpit, with a double staircase and a superb chancel screen, both the work of George Gilbert Scott, who designed them for the restoration work which was

begun in 1857. The south transept was built in 1230, although the great window is later, and here are displayed the colours of the Staffordshire Regiment. The regimental chapel is here too.

Lichfield Cathedral has a magnificent west front, containing 113 statues of kings, queens and other figures, mostly produced during the nineteenth century. Around the cathedral are some superb half-timbered buildings dating from the fourteenth to the seventeenth centuries, notably the Bishop's Palace, which is now the cathedral choir school.

Lichfield: St Mary

A short walk from the cathedral is the guild church of St Mary, in Market Square, with an imposing statue of Dr Johnson outside. The building has been converted to house the city's Heritage Exhibition (see chapter 7) although the Dyott Chapel is retained for worship.

Lichfield Cathedral.

Lichfield: St Michael

The original church of St Michael on Greenhill, in Church Street, was built in the thirteenth century, with the tower and spire added in the next century. Its churchyard is said to be one of the biggest in England and was listed in the sixteenth century as being one of the original Christian burial grounds in the city.

Rugeley: St Augustine

The oldest building in Rugeley is the former parish church of St Augustine. Now known as the Old Chancel, it consists of the tower, chancel and north chapel of a church that was originally founded in about 1150. However, most of what stands today is of the thirteenth century, with the tower from the fourteenth. The chancel includes a window of 1300.

A new parish church, also dedicated to St Augustine, was built between 1819 and 1823, generally in the Perpendicular style. The east end was added in 1905-6 and in this and in the north chapel there is stained glass by Kempe.

Dominating the town centre skyline, is the Roman Catholic church of Saints Joseph and Ethelreda, built in 1849 to a massive scale. A high, slender spire springs from the parapet of a fine tower, and of particular note is the bell of 1546 from Gloucestershire.

Rushton Spencer: St Laurence

This moorland church is an isolated building standing on a hilltop site. It was built of gritstone and slate during the seventeenth and eighteenth centuries. There is a boarded bell turret and an extremely rare thirteenth-century timbered nave with heavy pillars like massive tree trunks. The church also has a minstrel's gallery, a Jacobean pulpit, a squire's pew and several fittings which are more domestic than ecclesiastical in their nature.

Stafford: St Mary

At the time of the Norman Conquest, Stafford is said to have had a church with thirteen priests. It is not known whether this was the tenth-century church of St Bertelin or the first St Mary's church, lying immediately to its east. The first surviving portion of St Mary's, the nave and crossing, was erected around 1206, and the church had a college of canons which survived until 1546. St Mary's became a normal parish church in the sixteenth century and remains so today, standing in the heart of the town. Its windows portray much

of the town's early history, and the Norman font has carvings of human and animal figures. The church was extensively restored by George Gilbert Scott between 1840 and 1845.

Stone

Stone is said to derive its name from a cairn erected over the bodies of the princes Wulfid and Rufin, two of Britain's earliest Christian martyrs. The Augustinians founded a priory in Stone in the twelfth century but only one arch and some cloisters remain today. The present parish church dates from 1750 and contains several interesting monuments, including a bust of Admiral Earl St Vincent, the hero of the great naval victory off Cape St Vincent in 1797. Other interesting features of the church include stained glass windows depicting the martyrs Wulfid and Rufin.

Tamworth: St Editha

The Collegiate and Parish Church of St Editha, in the centre of Tamworth, stands on a site where there was certainly one Anglo-Saxon church, and possibly two. A church was founded in 963 but was rebuilt after the Norman Conquest and again after a disastrous fire in 1345. The church today retains Norman, Early English and later work of note. The crypt below the south aisle is oddly placed in relation to the nave and could, it is thought, have developed from a detached stone building. The fifteenth-century tower has an unusual double spiral staircase, with one staircase beginning in the churchyard, the other inside the church.

Walsall: St Matthew

St Matthew's church, with its soaring 170 foot (52 metre) high spire, is one of the most distinctive landmarks in Walsall. The church is thought to date from the twelfth century and the crypt contains a bricked-up Norman doorway built around 1150. The church was originally known as All Saints but has been St Matthew's since the eighteenth century. In the south porch, the main entrance to the church, can be seen the contrast between the Bath stone which was used to encase the nave and tower during the nineteenth century and the local sandstone used for rebuilding and extending the church in the fifteenth century, which came from Brewood and Sandwell. There is some fine wood carving in the choir stalls, with well preserved figures and poppy heads on the armrests and bench ends.

Ford Green Hall, Smallthorn.

6
Historic buildings and gardens

The ancestral home of the Queen's cousin, a ruined mansion at the centre of one of the world's leading leisure parks and many other historic houses can be found within Staffordshire. Not far from Castle Ring on Cannock Chase are the ruins of Beaudesert, the splendid mansion of the Marquesses of Anglesey, which was pulled down between 1932 and 1935. It was said to have been a wonderful piece of architecture. All that remains of it is the early nineteenth-century lodge and a fragment of the Tudor great hall. Part of the estate is used as a golf course and part as a camp for scouts and guides, but it is not open to the general public.

North of the Trent is the stately home of Lady Nancy Bagot, Blithfield Hall. This is a magnificent house of the Elizabethan period with Georgian and Regency additions. The Bagots and their ancestors the de Blithfields have lived here since 1086. The house is built around a courtyard and stands in the lovely setting of its landscape garden, with the church in the background. Blithfield Hall is not open to the public, but many other fine houses in Staffordshire are. These are detailed here.

Alton Towers, Alton. Telephone: 0538 702200.

The ruined mansion is the former home of the Earls of Shrewsbury and its gardens and grounds include splendid collections of flowers and shrubs. It was in 1814 that the monumental task of laying out these gardens was begun by Charles, the fifteenth Earl. His talent for landscaping has seldom been equalled and when he died in 1827 the work was continued in magnificent style by his nephew John, the sixteenth Earl, who expanded the house out of all recognition, to justify its grand name of Alton Towers. The splendid gardens and stately buildings form the spectacular setting for the renowned Alton Towers Leisure Park (see chapter 8).

Biddulph Grange Garden, Biddulph, Stoke-on-Trent ST8 7SD. Telephone: 0782 513149. National Trust.

This rare survival of a high Victorian garden was acquired by the National Trust in 1988 and is being restored. Created by the owner James Bateman in the 1840s and 1850s, the 15 acres (6 ha) were divided into a number of smaller gardens and contained specimens from his extensive plant collection. The Egyptian court, Chinese pagoda and Willow Pattern bridge, pinetum and other settings present the visitor with a series of delightful surprises in a miniature tour of the world. There is a restaurant.

Chillington Hall, near Wolverhampton. Telephone: 0902 850236. 2 miles (3 km) south-west of Brewood.

Chillington Hall is a Georgian-style house superbly set in grounds created by Capability Brown. The Giffard family came to Chillington in the twelfth century and built a castle. That has long since disappeared but the site has remained the seat of the Giffard family through the ensuing centries. The hall has some fine plasterwork and eighteenth-century furnishings. It is opened to the public, though not on a daily basis.

Dorothy Clive Garden, Willoughbridge. On A51 9 miles (14 km) south-west of Newcastle-under-Lyme.

Impressive particularly when the rhododendrons are out but lovely throughout the year, this 7 acre (2.8 ha) quarry garden in a fine landscaped setting has rock and scree

The Pagoda Fountain, Alton Towers.

gardens, rare trees, shrub roses and a water garden.

Ford Green Hall, Ford Green, Smallthorn, Stoke-on-Trent. Telephone: 0782 534771.

Ford Green Hall is a timber-framed farmhouse built around 1580 for the Ford family, well-to-do yeomen farmers who occupied the house until the end of the eighteenth century. During the two hundred years that the family lived there, various alterations were made to the building, following the changing fashions. The porch, for example, is a later addition and the asymmetrical brick wing was added around 1734 to replace the original timber-framed cross-wing.

Visitors are given a guided tour of the house and can see furniture including four-poster beds, long-case clocks, chests and cradles, as well as many kitchen utensils which have now passed out of use. The exhibits are of a type that the inhabitants of the house could well have used here between the sixteenth and eighteenth centuries.

Hanch Hall, Lichfield. Telephone: 0543 490308. 4 miles (6 km) north-west of Lichfield.

Situated roughly midway between Rugeley and Lichfield. Hanch Hall is a mansion of thirteenth-century origin which is now a mixture of Tudor, Jacobean, Queen Anne and Georgian architecture. The Queen Anne facade is very fine and the collections in the house include antique dolls, needlework, seventeenth-century parchments, costumes and teapots. There are Elizabethan cellars.

Hoar Cross Hall, Hoar Cross, Burton upon Trent. Telephone: 0283 75224.

Hoar Cross Hall is a nineteenth-century Elizabethan-style mansion set in 20 acres (8.1 ha) of woodland and gardens. The house has an imposing interior, together with some interesting items on display. Medieval-style banquets are held between September and June.

Moseley Old Hall, Wolverhampton. Telephone: 0902 782808.

Situated between the A449 and A460 a few miles north of Wolverhampton, Moseley Old Hall is a timber-framed house in which King Charles II was given refuge after the Battle of Worcester. The half-timbered walls are now enclosed in brick but inside there remains the

The knot garden at Moseley Old Hall, Wolverhampton, was created from a seventeenth-century design.

four-poster bed where the king slept and the surroundings are just as they were on the occasion of his flight from the battle. The garden features period plants and a seventeenth-century box parterre.

Oak House, Oak Road/Cambridge Street, West Bromwich. Telephone: 021-553 0759.

Oak House is a Tudor timber-framed yeoman's house, furnished in period style with a fine collection of oak furniture of the sixteenth and seventeenth centuries.

Shugborough, Milford, Stafford. Telephone: 0889 881388. 4 miles (6 km) south of Stafford on the A513.

Shugborough's mansion house and estate have been the home of the Anson family since 1624. Today it is the home of the Earl of Lichfield, cousin of the Queen. The house has connections with the famous Admiral George Anson, First Sea Lord in the mid eighteenth century. Shugborough is owned by the National Trust, but administered on the Trust's behalf by Staffordshire County Council, which has developed it as the county museum and as a popular place to visit for

leisure and education.

The house contains a fine collection of eighteenth-century ceramics, silver, pictures and French furniture, and is staffed by knowledgeable guides. The formal terraced lawns to the west of the house were laid out in 1855. Together with the banks of the river Sow, the rose garden and the less formal gardens, they form a delightful backcloth to the eighteenth-century garden monuments: the Chinese House, the Cat's Monument, the Classical Ruin, the Shepherd's Monument and the Doric Temple.

The landscaped park contains other monuments of great importance in the evolution of English architecture in the eighteenth century. The Temple of the Winds, the Triumphal Arch and the Lanthorn of Demosthenes were designed by James Stuart and are among the earliest buildings in England in the neo-classical style.

The domestic buildings at Shugborough house **Staffordshire County Museum** in the restored estate interiors, including the brewhouse, coach houses and laundry, and a reconstructed tailor's shop from Abbots Bromley, a general village store from Yoxall and exhibitions of domestic life, costume, toys and traditional and contemporary crafts.

A quarter of a mile (400 metres) away from the house, **Shugborough Park Farm** has been restored as a museum working farm, recreating nineteenth-century agricultural life. The farm was originally built around 1805 as the home farm to the estate. Today there are displays of farm machinery and farm animals of local and other rare breeds can be seen. These include Tamworth pigs, Bagot goats, Longhorn and White Park cattle, Shropshire sheep, Shire horses and poultry. Traditional farming methods are demonstrated to the public, including butter and cheese making in the dairy, hand milking in the milking parlour and cart work with the Shire horses. Displays enable visitors to spot the queen bee in the beehive in the Cottager's Life Gallery, watch the grinders and crushers at work in the old cornmill, and see how tractors first took over the hard manual work of haymaking.

Special farm working weekends are held, with each event highlighting a particular seasonal activity, for example spinning and shearing at Easter and threshing at harvest time. Craftsmen and women demonstrate rural crafts and skills such as beekeeping, hedge laying and farriery, and local enthusiasts display items like vintage tractors and engines or perform folk dances. Other special events are put on throughout the year.

Trentham Gardens, Trentham, Stoke-on-Trent. Telephone: 0782 657341. On the A34 south of Stoke.

Here there are beautiful gardens, historic buildings, craft shops, a park and woodland, with fishing, boating, amusements and many other attractions, situated in 800 acres (324 ha) of woodland. Country sports and activities ranging from go-karting to caravanning also take place here. Trentham was formerly the home of the Dukes of Sutherland.

Weston Park, near Shifnal. Telephone: 095276 207. 5 miles (8 km) north-east of Shifnal on the A5.

Weston Park is the handsome mansion of

Shugborough.

Trentham Gardens.

the Earl of Bradford, an early Restoration house built by Lady Wilbraham in 1671, and a superb example of this period of architecture. Weston houses a fine art collection, including works by Holbein, Van Dyck, Bassano, Reynolds, Gainsborough and Stubbs. The 1000 acres (400 ha) of grounds were laid out by Capability Brown and in-

clude some magnificent trees. Attractions which broaden the appeal of the traditional 'stately home' include nature trails, an architectural trail, rare breeds of farm livestock, a miniature steam railway and free flying exotic birds.

Wightwick Manor, Wolverhampton. Telephone: 0902 761108.

This Victorian manor house was built in 1887 and is a notable example of the influence of William Morris, the nineteenth-century poet and craftsman. The house is now in the care of the National Trust and contains many original Morris wallpapers and fabrics and Pre-Raphaelite works of art, as well as glass by Kempe and tiles by de Morgan. The gardens are notable for their yew hedges and topiary terraces.

Wolseley Garden Park, Rugeley. Telephone: 0889 574888.

More than 40 acres (16 ha) of ornamental gardens are said to be the first on a grand scale to be developed privately for opening to the public. There are lakeside walks, an archaeological dig, a garden centre and a maze in the shape of Britannia.

Wightwick Manor.

A delivery van at the Bass Museum, Burton upon Trent.

7
Museums and art galleries

ABBOTS BROMLEY
Puppet Theatre Museum, Edinburgh House, Bagot Street, Abbots Bromley. Telephone: 0283 840348.

Over two hundred delightful and unusual puppets from Victorian times up to the present may be seen on Sunday afternoons and by groups by appointment.

BARLASTON
Wedgwood Museum and Visitor Centre. See chapter 8.

BURTON UPON TRENT
Bass Museum, Visitor Centre and Shire Horse Stables, Horninglow Street, Burton upon Trent. Telephone: 0283 511000.

This museum, opened in 1977 during the bicentenary of Bass, the brewers, is situated in the former Bass joiners' shop, which has been restored and houses several exhibitions. Features include a model of Burton as it was in 1921, an experimental Brew House, a reconstructed Edwardian bar and 'Bass – the Company Story'. The Bass historic fleet of horse-drawn and motorised vehicles is on view as are the Bass Shire horses.

Burton upon Trent became a brewing centre because of the special qualities of its water, derived from the carboniferous limestone and gypsum of the southern Pennines. The modern brewing industry expanded during the eighteenth century, with the opening of the Trent and Mersey Canal. This gave the town links with the ports of Liverpool and Hull. Bass set up his first brewery in Burton just a year after the completion of the canal. Others followed, and six major breweries operate in the town today.

Heritage Brewery Museum, Anglesey Road, Burton upon Trent. Telephone: 0283 69226.

One of the largest collections of bottled beers in Britain is here, together with the story of the craft of traditional ale-brewing, housed in a typical Victorian brewery. It is the first independent working brewery museum.

CHEDDLETON
Cheddleton Flint Mill, Leek Road, Cheddleton, Leek. Telephone: Leek Tourist Information Centre, 0538 399181 or 381000.

Two mills are preserved in working order with their waterwheel, beside the Caldon Canal at Cheddleton. The museum includes a collection of machinery used in grinding flints for use in the manufacture of pottery, a steam engine, model engine and narrow boat.

Stoke-on-Trent City Museum and Art Gallery.

Cheddleton Railway Centre, Cheddleton Station, Leek. Telephone: 0538 360522.

The Victorian station is a listed building and there are steam and diesel locomotives as well as coaches and other rolling stock, and a small museum. Short steam-hauled rides can be enjoyed on Sundays in summer.

ECCLESHALL
Izaak Walton Cottage, Shallowford, near Eccleshall. Telephone: 0785 760278.

Izaak Walton is remembered best as the author of *The Compleat Angler*. His attractive cottage is in the heart of the Staffordshire countryside, between Stafford and Eccleshall. A period herb garden has been established and picnic facilities and refreshments are available.

Mill Meece Pumping Station, Mill Meece, near Eccleshall. Telephone: 0270 873683.

This early twentieth-century steam-powered water pumping station houses engines of several types including two horizontal steam engines. The engines are steamed on special days.

LEEK
Brindley Mill and James Brindley Museum, Mill Street, Leek. Telephone: 0538 384195.

This is a restored eighteenth-century water-powered corn mill providing small quantities of flour. The mill was built by James Brindley, who was renowned as a canal engineer and is regarded as one of the fathers of the industrial revolution. There is a museum, illustrating his life and times and the craft of millwrighting.

Leek Art Gallery, Nicholson Institute, Leek ST13 6DW. Telephone: 0538 385181.

This is a small art gallery, frequently supplemented by exhibitions. There is a collection of maps and objects of local interest, with a permanent exhibition of embroidery and paintings.

LICHFIELD
Lichfield Art Gallery, Lichfield Library, The Friary, Lichfield. Telephone: 0543 262177.

Various exhibitions are held in the year.

Lichfield Heritage Exhibition and Treasury, St Mary's Centre, Lichfield. Telephone: 0543 256611.

The exhibition portrays the fascinating and exciting history of Lichfield, through displays which include a magnificent selection of civic, church and regimental plate. An audio-visual presentation shows how the Civil War played a part in the city's history.

Museum of the Staffordshire Regiment (Prince of Wales's), Whittington Barracks, Lichfield. Telephone: 0543 433333 extension 3229/3240. 3 miles (5 km) south-east of Lichfield.

The museum contains many interesting

items from the former North and South Staffordshire Regiments. Included are relics from the Sikh Wars, the Crimea, the Indian Mutiny, the Zulu War, Egypt, Sudan, South Africa and both World Wars. The display of medals includes seven of the thirteen Victoria Crosses awarded to members of the regiment.

Samuel Johnson Birthplace Museum, Breadmarket Street, Lichfield WS13 6LG. Telephone: 0543 264972.

The house in which Samuel Johnson, the writer and lexicographer, was born in 1709 is a museum of his life, works and personality. It contains furniture, books, pictures and other items associated with the man who was one of the dominant figures of the eighteenth century. There is also an important collection of books and manuscripts on Johnson and his age. The house is the headquarters of the international Johnson Society.

NEWCASTLE-UNDER-LYME
Newcastle Borough Museum and Hobbergate Art Gallery, Brampton Park, Newcastle-under-Lyme ST5 0QP. Telephone: 0782 619705.

The gallery and museum house a collection of charters and examples of merchandise produced during the industrial revolution. The town's local history collection includes ceramics and firearms.

SHUGBOROUGH
Staffordshire County Museum and Mansion House, Shugborough, Milford, Staffordshire. Telephone: 0889 881388.

This museum of Staffordshire life and Shugborough Park Farm are described under *Shugborough* in chapter 6.

STAFFORD
Ancient High House, Greengate Street, Stafford. Telephone: 0785 40204.

This is the largest timber-framed town house in England, built in 1595. It is now a visitor centre and houses a permanent collection of furniture, paintings and costume as well as heritage exhibitions, the tourist information centre and a shop.

16th/5th The Queen's Royal Lancers and Staffordshire Yeomanry Regimental Museum, Kitchener House, Lammascote Road, Stafford ST16 3TA. Telephone: 0785 45840.

Kitchener House contains relics of the 5th Royal Irish Lancers, 16th The Queen's Own Lancers, 16th/5th The Queen's Royal Lancers and the Staffordshire Yeomanry from 1790.

Stafford Art Gallery and Craft Shop, Lichfield Road, Stafford. Telephone: 0785 53703.

Stafford Art Gallery has a varied programme of exhibitions of contemporary art, craft, photography and local history. The craft shop stocks the work of many new and leading British craftsmen and women.

William Salt Library, Eastgate Street, Stafford ST16 2LZ. Telephone: 0785 52276.

An eighteenth-century town house contains a comprehensive and valuable collection of books, drawings, engravings and documents of Staffordshire history.

STOKE-ON-TRENT
Chatterley Whitfield Mining Museum, Tunstall, Stoke-on-Trent ST6 8UN. Telephone: 0782 813337.

The winner of the 1982 Museum of the Year Award for the best industrial museum in Britain, Chatterley Whitfield gives the visitor the opportunity to descend to an underground gallery and see local mining techniques old and new, guided by former miners. Also on display are the steam winding engine, locomotives and pit ponies.

Etruria Industrial Museum, Lower Bedford Street, Etruria, Stoke-on-Trent. Telephone: 0782 287557.

Jesse Shirley's Etruscan Bone and Flint Mill was built to grind materials for agriculture and the pottery industry. The only surviving steam-powered potters' mill, complete with a working 1820 beam engine, which is periodically steamed, provides the basis of the industrial museum to be established here.

Gladstone Pottery Museum, 26 Uttoxeter Road, Longton, Stoke-on-Trent ST3 1PQ. Telephone: 0782 319232.

Museum of the Year in 1972, this is a working museum of British pottery. Housed in a complete, preserved nineteenth-century pottery with all the appropriate machinery and equipment, it tells the story of ceramics with a variety of pottery wares and demonstrations.

Stoke-on-Trent City Museum and Art Gallery, Bethesda Street, Hanley, Stoke-on-Trent ST1 3DW. Telephone: 0782 202173.

This is one of the finest museums in Britain and a former winner of the Museum of the Year award. It has one of the finest and largest collections of pottery and porcelain in the world. The ceramics galleries tell the fascinating story of pots and potters in chronological sequence, showing the importance and expansion of the city of Stoke-on-Trent as the centre of English ceramics production from the seventeenth century to the present day.

The Fine Art section puts on regularly changing exhibitions housed in three separate galleries. Two have been designed to be totally flexible, enabling them to be used for art forms ranging from the traditional to the avant-garde, and the third is an unusual indoor Sculpture Court visible from all levels in the museum.

The Decorative Arts Gallery shows costume, textiles, glass, oriental antiques, furniture, jewellery and enamels. The display follows a chronological sequence using the influence of various art forms, particularly the eastern impact on European art, to illustrate changes in style over the centuries to the present day. Low light levels enhance the beauty of the exhibits.

The Natural History Gallery presents the major habitats of Staffordshire and their associated rocks, plants and animals. Where possible, areas are unglazed, allowing a better view of the exhibits. Examples of rocks and vertebrate animals are on display, encouraging visitors to touch, thus making the gallery a firm favourite with children.

The Social History Gallery provides glimpses of Stoke-on-Trent's more recent past and concentrates on the common objects of the everyday life of the working people of the Potteries. There is a typical terrace-type living room, a wash-house, chemist's shop, fish and chip shop range and counter, and a public house bar. There is a complete Spitfire aircraft, to commemorate its local designer.

The Archaeology Gallery displays include Staffordshire sites of all periods from the mesolithic to the eighteenth century and range from a cave shelter to a Cistercian abbey. The bias towards the post-medieval period is a result of so much archaeological work being directed towards understanding the origins and growth of the local ceramics industry.

TAMWORTH

Tamworth Castle Museum, Tamworth. Telephone: 0827 311222 or 63563 (weekends).

For details of this museum, see under Tamworth Castle in chapter 4.

WALSALL

Birchills Canal Museum, Top Lock, Old Birchills Road, Walsall. Telephone: 0922 653175.

The lives of the people who worked on them and the history of the canals around Walsall are recorded in the displays in this former Boatmen's Rest and Mission. There are canal memorabilia of all descriptions and a replica boat cabin.

Jerome K. Jerome Birthplace Museum, Belsize House, Bradford Street, Walsall WS1 1PN. Telephone: 0922 653135.

Jerome K. Jerome, author of *Three Men in a Boat*, is one of Walsall's most famous sons, although he lived in the town for only two years, and this museum is in the house where he was born. Jerome returned to Walsall to be awarded the freedom of the borough in the 1920s, shortly before he died. The central library in the town also has an extensive collection of material about him.

Walsall Leather Centre Museum, 56-57 Wisemore, Walsall. Telephone: 0922 721153.

This fascinating working museum, which won the National Heritage Museum of the Year Award in 1990, is housed in a Victorian factory in the British centre of the leather trade. Displays show all the stages of leather production and craftsmen and craftswomen demonstrate the skills of leather working in faithfully reproduced workshops. There is a café and a gift shop.

Walsall Museum and Art Gallery, Lichfield Street, Walsall WS1 1TR. Telephone: 0922 650000 extension 3124.

The story of the development of Walsall through the ages is told here in words, photographs and exhibits, with a special emphasis on the town's traditional trades of iron and leather. Walsall's famous citizens Jerome K. Jerome and Sister Dora, the Florence Nightingale of the industrial revolution, are remembered too. Many interesting items from Walsall's past are on show including the old market bell, truncheons from the early days of the police force and a ballista ball used in the siege of Rushall Hall during the Civil War.

The Garman-Ryan Collection was donated by the widow of the sculptor Sir Jacob Epstein to the Walsall Museum in 1974. Lady Epstein was born in the West Midlands and wanted the collection to remain there on display. The collection is a diverse one, ranging from a Dürer woodcut to a Picasso etching, while the paintings, drawings and sculptures by Sir Jacob Epstein are the most representative collection of his work in Britain. It also includes work by Blake, Rembrandt, Matisse, Augustus John, Constable, Reynolds, Turner and Van Gogh, and there are works of art from ancient Greece, Egypt, China, Africa, Polynesia and the Middle East.

WEDNESBURY
Art Gallery and Museum, Holyhead Road, Wednesbury. Telephone: 021-556 0683.

Founded in 1891, the Art Gallery is based round a collection of pictures bequeathed by the widow of a local resident. The Ruskin Pottery Collection is also here and galleries devoted to the geology of the Black Country and the nineteenth-century travels of a West Bromwich lady. Other exhibitions are mounted regularly.

WILLENHALL
The Lock Museum, 54 New Road, Willenhall. Telephone: 0902 634542.

This Victorian lockmaker's house and workshop are typical of the small family businesses which flourished in Willenhall. Visitors can see locks being made by skilled craftsmen and there are displays of locks and keys. The way in which a lockmaking family lived is shown in a series of period rooms. This is a fascinating and unusual little museum.

Willenhall Museum, Willenhall Library, Walsall Street, Willenhall. Telephone: 0902 653175.

Lockmaking was the special skill of the people of Willenhall and this museum illustrates the history and social life of the community.

WOLVERHAMPTON
Bantock House Museum, Bantock Park, Bradmore Road, Wolverhampton WV3 9LQ. Telephone: 0902 312132.

A mile or so south-west of the centre of Wolverhampton lie the 43 acres (17 ha) of Bantock Park. In these pleasant surroundings stands Bantock House Museum. The

The Garman-Ryan Collection, Walsall Museum and Art Gallery.

house, its contents and its grounds were bequeathed to the town in 1938 by Alderman A. Baldwin Bantock, a former mayor and honorary alderman, in whose honour the house, formerly known as Merridale House, and its grounds were renamed.

The museum provides Wolverhampton's main displays of decorative art. Its pottery and porcelain collection includes fine examples from various British factories like Worcester and Wedgwood. The museum has a large collection of dolls and toys, from the 1780s to the 1930s. Bantock House is also known for its historic collections of japanning and enamelling, the two decorative art industries of the eighteenth and nineteenth centuries which are particularly associated with the Wolverhampton area. In these respects Bantock House is a museum of national importance and has been described as one of the finest small museums in Europe. There are formal gardens in the grounds.

Bilston Art Gallery and Museum, Mount Pleasant, Bilston, Wolverhampton WV14 7LU. Telephone: 0902 409143.

This museum is primarily devoted to local history and the strong influence of the industrial revolution on the development of the area. Particularly notable is the world-famous collection of Bilston enamels, which is on permanent display. On the ground floor of the building is the art gallery, which mounts a varied programme of temporary exhibitions, often featuring the work of local artists.

Wolverhampton Art Gallery and Museum, Lichfield Street, Wolverhampton WV1 1DU. Telephone: 0902 312032.

The gallery is housed in an imposing Victorian building opened in 1884. A good collection has been built up and many of its paintings and sculptures are on permanent display in the first-floor rooms. These include works by Gainsborough, Wilson, Fuseli, Wright of Derby, Zoffany, Landseer and the local artist Edward Bird, as well as many more British artists of the eighteenth and nineteenth centuries. The gallery has outstanding collections of oriental decorative art and British and American 'pop art', alongside a gallery which is reserved for temporary exhibitions. The 'Wolverhampton Room' is devoted to local history.

The craft shop, Stafford Art Gallery

The Wedgwood craft centre, Barlaston.

8
Other places to visit

POTTERY MUSEUMS AND FACTORY VISITS

Since the early eighteenth century, Stoke-on-Trent has been the centre of the British ceramic industry. Important collections of English pottery and porcelain are displayed at the City Museum and Art Gallery, and the Gladstone Pottery Museum preserves a complete nineteenth-century pottery (see chapter 7). Some old and famous firms have museums or visitor centres and also provide guided tours around their factories. It is important to book most tours in advance. These firms have factory shops, as do many others in the city: visitors should enquire at the tourist information centre (telephone: 0782 411222) or at the City Museum (telephone: 0782 202173).

John Beswick (Royal Doulton), Gold Street, Longton, Stoke-on-Trent. Telephone: 0782 313041.

Here fine ceramic sculptures have been created for over a century. They include life-like studies of horses, farm and other animals and Beatrix Potter characters as well as the well known character and Toby jugs. The artists and craftspeople who make them can be seen at work. It is essential to book the tour in advance. Children under fourteen are not allowed.

Coalport, Minerva Works, Park Street, Fenton, Stoke-on-Trent. Telephone: 0782 45274.

The guided tour, which must be booked in advance, shows the visitor the processes in the manufacture of Coalport fine bone china. There is a craft centre where demonstrations are given of traditional pottery skills. Children under thirteen are not admitted.

Heron Cross Pottery Visitor Centre, Chilton Street, Fenton, Stoke-on-Trent. Telephone: 0782 599748.

The visitor centre is housed in a restored Victorian potbank with a bottle oven which now houses a unique kiln and craft centre. Hand-thrown terracotta pots are among the items for sale and there is a restaurant.

Minton (Royal Doulton), London Road, Stoke-on-Trent. Telephone: 0782 744766.

'The world's most beautiful china' has been made since 1793. Today visitors can see the processes involved in making fine bone china and watch the skilful artists engaged in hand-painting and decorating many wares. It is im-

33

portant to book tours in advance. In the museum the history of the company can be traced through the range of historic wares displayed, pattern books and other records. Children under twelve are not admitted.

Moorcroft, Sandbach Road, Cobridge, Stoke-on-Trent. Telephone: 0782 24323.

The restored bottle oven, in which pottery used to be fired, can be seen above the factory where on Wednesdays visitors who book in advance are shown the hand-made ornamental pottery in production. There is a museum.

Royal Doulton, Nile Street, Burslem, Stoke-on-Trent. Telephone: 0782 575454.

Tours of the factory show all stages in the manufacture of the famous fine bone china figures and tableware, from the automatic plate-making machines and the delicate work of making tiny flowers for china ladies to the deft hand-painting of important pieces. It is essential to book in advance. The Sir Henry Doulton Gallery, open to all visitors, houses the company's collection of historic figures, early wares, sketches, pattern books and so on, and illustrates the story of Doulton from its beginning in Lambeth in 1814 to today. Children under twelve are not admitted.

Royal Grafton China, Marlborough Road, Longton, Stoke-on-Trent. Telephone: 0782 599667.

All the stages in the manufacture of china tableware and gift ware can be seen on the extensive guided tour, which should be booked in advance.

Spode, Church Street, Stoke-on-Trent. Telephone: 0782 744011.

The unique Spode collection of earthenware, bone china and stoneware can be seen in the Spode Museum at the beginning of the factory tour (by appointment only), when visitors are shown the processes in the production of bone china. Children under twelve are not allowed.

Wedgwood Museum and Visitor Centre, Josiah Wedgwood and Sons Limited, Barlaston, Stoke-on-Trent ST12 9ES. Telephone: 0782 204141.

The centre houses an extensive collection of the products of Josiah Wedgwood, the pottery manufacturers, from 1750 to the present day. Wedgwood have also re-created the eighteenth-century Wedgwood workshops at Etruria, complete with a reconstructed bottle kiln and an original engine turning lathe, which is still in use today. The display shows vividly the working conditions of those times. The visitor can look at more than two centuries of the company's history, with rooms designed to recapture the style of specific periods, containing hundreds of Wedgwood pieces from those eras. The visitor can watch potters and decorators at work using traditional skills to create today's Wedgwood products. There is a cinema, refreshment lounge and a souvenir shop.

OTHER ATTRACTIONS

Alton Towers, Alton. Telephone: 0538 702200.

Set in 800 acres (324 ha) of grounds, this claims to be Europe's premier leisure park. There are over 125 rides and attractions, including spectacular rides like 'Black Hole', 'Grand Canyon' and 'Thunder-Looper Rollercoaster', and special events throughout the year. See also chapter 6.

Amerton Working Farm, Stowe-by-Chartley, near Weston. Telephone: 0889 270294.

Visitors can watch all aspects of the daily work involved with a pedigree Jersey herd of cows, as well as cheese and ice-cream making. There are shops, a bakery and a cafe.

Blackbrook Farm Animal World and Shetland Centre, Winkhill, near Leek. Telephone: 0538 308293.

Rare breeds of sheep and goats, together with deer, llamas, chipmunks and other animals, are reared here. Displays of shearing and spinning are given and hand-spun woollen goods are for sale.

Brooklyn Farm and Craft Workshop, Waterfall, Waterhouses, Stoke-on-Trent. Telephone: 0538 308462.

British Friesland milking sheep provide the wool for the woven rugs and other goods made here as well as milk for the yoghurt and cheese.

The Children's Farm, Ash End House Farm, Middleton Lane, Middleton, near Tamworth. Telephone: 021-329 3240.

Here children are each given a small bucket

of food to feed the animals with as they go around the farm to look at the farm animals, rare breeds and Shire horses. They then may have a pony ride. There are play areas and picnic barns and a farm shop.

Drayton Manor Park and Zoo, Tamworth. Telephone: 0827 287979. 2 miles (3 km) south of Tamworth.

Set in 160 acres (65 ha) of attractive parkland and lakes, Drayton Manor Park and Zoo are centred on the former home of Tamworth's most famous Member of Parliament, Sir Robert Peel. The amusement park has over 45 attractions from roller-coasters and sky-flyers to children's rides. In the zoo a wide collection of animals are exhibited in the open-plan style, while there are nature trails, a garden centre and shops and restaurants.

Foxfield Steam Railway, Caverswall Road Station, Blythe Bridge, Stoke-on-Trent. Telephone: 0782 396210 or 314532.

The old colliery railway to Foxfield Colliery has been preserved and at weekends operates a passenger service. There are thirteen industrial locomotives here and a fascinating collection of old passenger vehicles.

Georgian Crystal Company, Silk Mill Lane, Tutbury. Telephone: 0238 814534.

The glassworks is down a small lane near the town centre and visitors can see the glass being blown and decorated as they go in.

Moorlands Farm Park, Upper Greenhills Farm, Ipstones Edge, Stoke-on-Trent. Telephone: 0538 266479.

1000 feet (300 metres) up in the spectacular Staffordshire Moorlands, the Moorlands Farm Park contains a wide range of rare breeds of British farm animals, many of which have been forced out of commercial farming by changes in taste, economics and fashion. Breeds at the farm include the spectacular Longhorn cattle, the ancient Soay sheep and Tamworth pigs. There are also picnic areas.

Private Museum of Prams, Wild Rock, The Common, Dilhorne, Stoke-on-Trent. Telephone: 0782 396301.

It is well worth making the necessary appointment to see the remarkable collection of prams and baby carriages, some of which date from the early nineteenth century.

Ridware Arts Centre, Hamstall Hall, Hamstall Ridware. Telephone: 088922 351.

Housed in an ancient building at Hamstall Hall, a lovely setting, are exhibition workshops, a craft shop and a restaurant.

Sandwell Park Farm Visitors' Centre, Salters Lane, West Bromwich. Telephone: 021-553 0020 or 2147.

Situated in Sandwell Valley Country Park, this home farm has been restored to operate as a nineteenth-century working farm museum. As well as rare breeds of livestock there are exhibitions about work on the farm and displays of old farm machinery.

Tutbury Crystal Glass, Burton Street, Tutbury. Telephone: 0238 813281.

The ancient craft of glassmaking still thrives in Tutbury and visitors can see craftsmen at work here on tours of the works.

Uttoxeter Heritage Centre, Carter Street, Uttoxeter. Telephone: 0889 567176.

The development of the town is reflected in changing displays at the centre housed in restored timber-framed cottages with a walled garden. There is a nineteenth-century cottage bedroom and a delightful Edwardian shop window.

Valley Heritage Centre, Valley Road, Hednesford. Telephone: 0543 877666.

Mining was once an important part of life in the valley and this centre, situated on an old mining site, illustrates the social, industrial and natural history of the area, with permanent and temporary exhibitions. Craft workers demonstrate their skills in the workshop and there is a cafe.

A trip on the Caldon Canal.

9
Canal county

Staffordshire has more miles of canals within its boundaries than any other county in England. Being at the heartland of England during the industrial revolution, Staffordshire's canals grew as industry grew. Even in the seventeenth century, when most of Staffordshire was agricultural, there was already a pottery industry in the north of the county. Early records described Burslem as being cratered with potholes and coal holes, with its inhabitants digging clay and coal in the backyards of their houses and fashioning rough earthenware pots which they baked in small home-made ovens.

This primitive craft the great potters of the eighteenth century transformed into an industry of international importance. An important factor in the industry's growth was the excellent communications which the canal system brought to Staffordshire. For while the north of the county enjoyed the natural advantage of the close proximity of useful clays and coal, Staffordshire's roads were inadequate and its rivers unnavigable for the sort of transport needed by the potters.

To make the fine pottery that was to be the basis of his fortune, Josiah Wedgwood needed to be able to bring to his Etruria factory cargoes of better quality clay, notably from Cornwall. Wedgwood promoted schemes of road construction but more importantly, with the farsightedness which was one of the reasons for his success, he commissioned the local engineer James Brindley to create the Trent and Mersey Canal. This enabled kaolin (china clay) to be brought by water right to the side of the Etruria factory and, equally important, the finished pottery could be taken away smoothly, with the minimum of breakages, to its markets.

Although the canals of Staffordshire no longer serve as a vital lifeline for the county's manufacturing industry, they have happily not fallen into disrepair and now serve the new and growing industry of leisure and tourism. Staffordshire's canals provide superb opportunities to explore the countryside, either by boat or by a gentle stroll along the towpath. Boating holidays are becoming increasingly popular, with many holidaymakers choosing a Staffordshire base for their holiday exploring the waterways of the north-west Midlands.

Staffordshire, at the hub of the English canal system, has many well equipped hiring fleets and is one of the best located and most convenient areas for a canal holiday. A good two-week holiday cruise is the 'ring' formed by the Trent and Mersey, the Staffordshire and Worcestershire and the Shropshire Union canals, but shorter trips are possible. Other ways of seeing the canals are by walking the towpaths or taking out a canoe, but remembering, in the latter case, the need for safety precautions.

Birmingham Canal Navigations

At Autherley Junction the main line of the Birmingham Canal Navigations joins the Staffordshire and Worcestershire Canal. This

Haywood Bridge, near Great Haywood.

network of waterways served the Black Country, bringing raw materials to the industrial villages that sprang up. Many noteworthy features survive. The most famous is probably the Dudley Tunnel, now restored. This was not only a through link but also served a network of underground canals to mine workings. Pleasure cruisers are not encouraged into the tunnel since the traverse is very long and hazardous, but special trip boats run from the Black Country Museum at its northern end to the Singing Cavern. Telephone Dudley Tunnel Trips (021-250 5321) for details.

Caldon Canal

The Caldon Canal joins the Trent and Mersey Canal at Etruria, Stoke-on-Trent, and was built to carry minerals from the uplands of the Peak District to the Potteries. The canal has been restored for pleasure craft, a magnificent section being through the Churnet valley.

There are many reminders of the early days of the industrial revolution along its banks, such as the remains of limekilns, ironstone workings and ironworks. Perhaps the best is the Flint Mill at Cheddleton, now restored as a museum of industrial archaeology (see chapter 7).

The Caldon's attractive setting can be experienced by taking one of the guided horse-drawn boat trips now run from the restored canalside warehouse at Froghall Wharf (see chapter 2). Telephone Wharf Passenger Services (0538 266486) for details.

Shropshire Union Canal

The Shropshire Union Canal, Telford's masterpiece, leaves the Staffordshire and Worcestershire Canal at Autherley Junction, near Wolverhampton, and, in its builder's typical fashion, runs north-west to Nantwich, often through deep cuttings, the most spectacular of which are at Norbury, with its famous high bridge, and at Tyrley, with its sheer rock sides. Further south near Brewood are two interesting works: the aqueduct over which Telford's canal crosses the same engineer's Holyhead Road (now the A5) and the ornamental bridge — or short tunnel — which he was obliged to construct to take the canal beneath the avenue to Chillington House. For information about pleasure cruises telephone Shropshire Union Cruises (0785 284292).

Staffordshire and Worcestershire Canal

One of the most beautiful canals, the Staffordshire and Worcestershire, with its characteristic round lock houses, leaves the Trent and Mersey at Great Haywood, from which there are sometimes excursions: telephone Vale of Trent Canal Cruises (0889 881328) for details. A lake, Tixall Wide, is crossed almost immediately and on the route south there are many delights including the Bratch, Brindley's famed flight of three locks near Wombourne, and the sandstone cuttings and ivy-covered tunnel near Stourton. The canal joins the river Severn at the eighteenth-century canal town of Stourport in the county of Hereford and Worcester.

Trent and Mersey Canal

This canal links the river Trent near Derby with the Mersey at Runcorn, a substantial part of its length being in Staffordshire. One of its many fine features is the Harecastle Tunnel, an amazing feat of engineering in the form of a tiny narrow hole through the hillside at Kidsgrove. In the first tunnel, some 2880 yards (2633 metres) long, and built by James Brindley in 1766-77, barges had to be 'legged' through the tunnel by men lying on their backs and pushing against the roof with their feet to give the boat momentum. Their horses took a route over the hill, still called Boathorse Road. When Thomas Telford modernised the canal in 1827 he overcame the bottleneck caused by the narrowness of Brindley's tunnel by building a new, wider tunnel alongside it, complete with a towpath. The northern portals of both tunnels can still be seen at Kidsgrove, just a short way from the station car park. While the towpath has now gone from Telford's tunnel, it is still used by pleasure boats, as is the whole canal. South of the Potteries, the Trent and Mersey runs close to the river Trent, passing the wild expanse of Cannock Chase and the busy Fradley Junction, where there is a connection to the Coventry Canal, before leaving Staffordshire by way of Burton upon Trent.

Abbots Bromley.

10
Towns and villages

ABBOTS BROMLEY

Abbots Bromley is best known for its annual Horn Dance, which is held there every September and claimed to be of prehistoric origin. The dance is possibly connected with obscure fertility rights but is more likely to have connections with privileges granted to the inhabitants of the Forest of Needwood, once a favourite royal hunting ground and in whose centre the village lay.

The day-long Horn Dance involves performances at the vicarage and throughout the village, and performers include a Hobby Horse, Maid Marion and a Jester. The dance starts at dawn outside the village church, makes a 20 mile (32 km) circuit of farms, where the dancers are welcomed as bearers of good fortune and fertility, and finishes in the main street of the village in the afternoon. It is enacted by six Deer-men, three of whom carry white and three black wooden replicas of reindeer heads attached to real antlers dating back into the mists of time. Music is provided by a melodeon player, while the Hobby Horse beats time with his jaws and the Bowman twangs his bowstring. The climax of the dance comes when the black and white Deer-men face each other and act out a mock combat, with their horns lowered.

The ceremony is thought to date back hundreds, maybe even thousands of years. Some say it is the remnant of a medieval pageant held to raise funds for the church, and the money raised during the day by the dancers is still used for this purpose. But others claim it predates Christianity and represents an ancient fertility rite, and the battle between light and darkness, or winter and spring. It may be that, when the Bowman stalks the Deer-men along the streets of Abbots Bromley, he is re-creating a ceremony meant to ensure the death of the reindeer and guarantee the survival of some prehistoric tribe that lived in the area.

Abbots Bromley is an interesting village, with more than forty buildings of architectural and historic interest. The ancient butter cross is particularly worth seeing and five pubs along the main street offer a welcome to visitors.

The parish church dates mostly from the thirteenth century and is particularly noted for its unusual lateral windows. The horns used in the Horn Dance are also kept there.

ALDRIDGE

Aldridge means 'the village among the alders' and today, despite its industrial nature and proximity to Walsall and the Black Country, it is still surrounded by fields and farms, although administratively it no longer lies within Staffordshire.

Aldridge was mentioned in the Domesday Book and for centuries was a heavily wooded part of the huge Cannock Forest. It was the industrial revolution that transformed it, with the mining of coal and the growth of brick and tile making. Then from the 1950s there was more growth as people and jobs were moved out of Birmingham and its immediate area.

A conservation area around Noddy Park, the Croft, the parish church of St Mary the Virgin and the Moot House protects the remaining parts of Aldridge's historical centre. The Hay Head Wood nature reserve is important primarily as a wildlife refuge, but it also has historical significance as it was once the site of the Hay Head lime works. The reserve covers about 13 acres (5.3 ha) and includes mixed woodland, scrub, grassland, marsh and open water habitats. Many wild plants and animals can be found and over fifty kinds of birds have been seen there.

The Alton lock-up.

ALREWAS

Bypassed by the A38, this attractive village should not be missed, with its many thatched black and white cottages. It gains much of its charm from its position by the waters of the river Trent and the Trent and Mersey Canal. Basket weaving and eel fishery were both thriving trades here.

ALSTONEFIELD

About 15 miles (24 km) due east of Leek, very close to the Derbyshire border, lies Alstonefield, a large village close to some of the most beautiful stretches of the Dove valley. The river here winds in a ravine beneath the hills, with wooded banks, weirs and falls and cliffside caves.

The parish church is a combination of Norman and Perpendicular architecture. The box pews and two-decker pulpit date from 1637. Alongside the church is the manor house, built in 1587 and now a farm. Only fragments now remain of the older Beresford Hall, where Charles Cotton, poet, essayist and part author, with Izaak Walton, of *The Compleat Angler*, stayed. Both men loved the river Dove and the famed Fishing House they built on its banks here still stands, bearing their initials carved over the door.

ALTON

The beautiful river Churnet flows through rich woodlands to join the Dove near Alton Towers, the great Gothic house built in 1809-23 by the elder Pugin for the fifteenth Earl of Shrewsbury, and said to have cost the Earl over one million pounds. This vast but now ruined house looks very romantic with its turrets, towers, battlements and pinnacles. Around the house is an 800 acre (324 ha) park that was landscaped by 'Capability' Brown and now forms the centrepiece of Alton Towers Leisure Park (see chapters 6 and 8).

In the village of Alton, the parish church has a fourteenth-century tower and Norman arcade. Nearby Alton Castle was built in 1847 to Pugin's designs but incorporating an earlier medieval tower. The rocky, wooded beauty of the scenery and the towers and castellated buildings have led to this part of the county being called the 'Rhineland of Staffordshire'.

ARMITAGE

South-east of Rugeley, the parish of Armitage with Handsacre is the home of

Alrewas parish church.

Armitage Shanks, the pottery manufacturers. The river Trent runs through Handsacre and is spanned by the High Bridge, a fine hundred-year-old iron bridge with a single span of 140 feet (43 metres). Nearby stand the four Ridwares, the villages of Hamstall Ridware (see chapter 8), Mavesyn Ridware, with the gatehouse to the hall of the de Mavesyn family, Pipe Ridware and Hill Ridware. In old English', *rydware* meant 'the place of the river folk'.

ASHLEY

Ashley is 9 miles (15 km) south-west of Newcastle-under-Lyme. Its church, while not spectacular in external appearance, contains magnificent interior work and monuments. The small village also has Catholic and Methodist churches.

AUDLEY

The history of Audley, near Newcastle-under-Lyme, began in Anglo-Saxon times. Originally it was a small farming community but coal mining began in the vicinity in the seventeenth century and the village began to grow. The period from 1840 to 1870 was the most significant in the development of the mining industry and consequently of the village.

BARLASTON

The massive Wedgwood factory in Barlaston lies close to the attractive village, just to the north of Stone. Barlaston Hall dates from the 1750s; a tall and imposing building, it is under restoration. The Wedgwood factory, set in superb estate surroundings, has a fine museum and visitor centre (see chapter 8).

BARTON-UNDER-NEEDWOOD

South-west of Burton-upon-Trent and close to the A38, Barton is a tidy village with a notable church, built in 1533 by Dr John Taylor, who became Master of the Rolls after service to King Henry VIII.

BETLEY

Betley lies to the north-west of Newcastle-under-Lyme in undulating wooded countryside. Its history stretches back to Anglo-Saxon times and the village is described in Domesday Book. Most of the village is designated as a conservation area.

BIDDULPH

Biddulph lies in the extreme north of Staffordshire, close to its border with Cheshire. The town has had a long history. After the Norman Conquest the manor was granted to

Brewood.

William by Robert the Forester, an overlord of what was then the extensively forested area of Lyme. Biddulph Grange belonged to the Cistercian monks of Abbey Hulton until the dissolution. The Biddulph family was staunchly Catholic and, in the Civil War, John Biddulph fought under the royal flag and was killed at the Battle of Hopton Heath. His son entrusted the defence of Biddulph Hall to Lord Brereton, who withstood a determined siege until 1644 when he was finally subjected to heavy artillery. The hall was then demolished to prevent its re-garrisoning. The unique nineteenth-century garden of a later house is open to the public (see chapter 6). In later years Biddulph became a strong centre of nonconformity, the meetings on Mow Cop (see chapter 2) in 1807 resulting in the establishment of Primitive Methodism. John Wesley visited Biddulph many times in those days.

BLOXWICH

Bloxwich is thought to have been uninhabited woodland at the time of the Domesday Book, though its name is probably Anglo-Saxon in origin. Now the town is part of the Metropolitan Borough of Walsall, having ceased administratively to be a part of Staffordshire in 1974. The metal trade has been carried on in Bloxwich since the late middle ages and by the second half of the eighteenth century it was, like Walsall, associated closely with the saddlers' ironmongery trade, making items such as stirrups and tack. Coal mining and brickmaking were industries that followed, encouraging more growth in the town.

Bloxwich's oldest monument is the medieval preaching cross in All Saints churchyard. Another point of historical interest is the mound of anvil stones in Short Heath Park. They were once used by metalworkers in the town and were erected as a monument. The park is the modern reminder of what was the village green.

BRANSTON

Close to Burton upon Trent, Branston can lay claim to a long history. There were Roman settlers here, and the village is mentioned periodically throughout recorded history. Relics of the mesolithic period (about nine thousand years ago) have been found preserved in one of the lagoons in the neighbourhood, which are now a haven for wildlife.

BRERETON

At the south-east end of Rugeley is Brereton, a mining village which has grown into a suburb. The Holly Bush, a former inn at Brereton Slade (Colliery Road), is an ancient timbered building. Brereton House dates from the late eighteenth century and Brereton Hall from the seventeenth century. The Cedar Tree Hotel is eighteenth-century with Regency-style bays added in the early nineteenth century. St Michael's church is described in chapter 5.

BREWOOD

Brewood is a small but busy market town of medieval origins, on the Shropshire Union Canal. It has an outstanding conservation area, with many fine buildings. These include the Tudor Brewood Hall and Blackladies, an old monastery, as well as a number of Queen Anne and early Georgian houses. Parts of the church of St Mary the Virgin and St Chad date back to the thirteenth century, while St Mary's Roman Catholic church, designed by Pugin, houses a statue of Our Lady of Brewood damaged by Cromwellian cannon fire.

BRIDGETOWN

This community lies between the A5 and A34 trunk roads and is a product of the industrial revolution. The old industries of edge-tool making, tilemaking and ironfounding have now been replaced by a variety of light industries.

BRINDLEY HEATH

Brindley Heath, towards the southern edge of Cannock Chase, consists almost wholly of wood and heathland, with the population scattered in small belts of housing on the edge. Much of the area is extremely beautiful and is a reminder that Cannock Chase is a designated Area of Outstanding Natural Beauty (see chapter 2). Some of the forest is under the control of the Forestry Commission and much of the country is at a high level, reaching 775 feet (236 metres) near Pye Green.

BURNTWOOD

Although part of Lichfield District, the township of Burntwood is as large as the city itself. It consists of three areas, Burntwood, Chasetown and Chase Terrace, and borders Cannock Chase and Chasewater. The small hamlets here grew during the late nineteenth century with the opening of the first coalpits in 1849 and the growth of a nail industry. Today the town is still expanding.

There are three Anglican churches in the Burntwood area: Christ Church at Burntwood was paid for by public subscription and consecrated in 1820; St Anne's church at Chasewater was erected in 1865 and is believed to have been the first church to be lit by electricity; and St John's.

BURTON UPON TRENT

Market days: Thursday, Friday and Saturday.

Burton is well known as the capital of brewing, having once been the home of over forty breweries. Brewing is still a major industry there but it is no longer so dominant. The rubber industry now rivals it as a major employer and other industries like engineering and joinery manufacture have arisen.

The administrative centre of East Staffordshire, Burton upon Trent lies on the A38 trunk road. The town has two major road bridges over the river Trent, one built in 1864, the second opened in 1985. Many buildings are reminders of the town's brewing history, notably the Bass Museum of Brewing History and the Heritage Brewery Museum (see chapter 7). Near the railway station is the magnificent Midland Railway Grain Warehouse, now splendidly restored and housing an information technology centre and other modern enterprises.

The Town Hall, further out of the town centre beyond the station, is a superb Gothic building (1894) fronted by an attractive square, on another side of which stands St Paul's church, completed in 1847, with its striking lines and central tower.

The town centre has a fine, atmospheric Victorian market hall and a bustling outdoor market, across the road from a pleasant modern shopping precinct.

See chapter 5 for St Modwen's church.

BUTTERTON

On the high moors east of Leek, Butterton is close to the Manifold valley and above the Hoo Brook. It is a compact village and on a very ancient site, although the church was rebuilt in 1872 and had a spire added in 1879.

CANNOCK

Market days Tuesday, Friday and Saturday.

On the southern edge of Cannock Chase lies the settlement known as 'Chenet' in the

Domesday Book. Today Cannock is centred around an attractive market place and its ancient bowling green framed by lime trees. Overlooking the green is the former Council House, an imposing Georgian house with a fine pair of ornamental gates. Nearby is the former conduit head building of the Cannock Conduit Trust, founded in 1736 to bring a water supply to the town. It supplied water until 1942. On the far side of the Market Place is St Luke's church, whose tower dates back to the fourteenth century (see chapter 5). The town has a good range of shops around Market Place and in the attractive precinct on Market Hall Street. Originally granted a market charter by Henry III in 1259, the town now has busy indoor and outdoor markets.

CAVERSWALL

A large parish on the east side of Stoke-on-Trent, Caverswall includes the village of that name as well as the agricultural communities of Caverswall Common and Roughcote. The village centres round its parish church, which has a Perpendicular tower and a long nave with an arcade rebuilt in the early seventeenth century, and its castle, built about 1614 on the site of a medieval castle.

Cheddleton Flint Mill.

CHEADLE

Market days Tuesday, Friday and Saturday.

Cheadle stands between Stoke-on-Trent and Uttoxeter and is a market and shopping centre for a wide area. In recent years the town has developed both residentially and commercially but not at the expense of history and tradition.

Cheadle was listed in the Domesday Book as 'Celle', a name that was derived, it is thought, from *ceorles* — merchants or traders. This long association with trade continued when Henry III granted the town privilege of holding a market or fair. By the time of Queen Elizabeth I Cheadle had almost two hundred houses and a number of these properties still stand as a fine group of black and white architecture.

By the late seventeenth century the town had assumed importance as the centre of a farming district, and coal mining was also developing in the area. In the 1830s the town was a centre for tape manufacture and close by there were extensive factories producing brass wire. Since then the town has more than doubled in size.

Elsewhere in Cheadle are a few timber-framed houses, several Georgian rows and at least one notable inn, the Wheatsheaf. The nearby market cross dates from the seventeenth century. In Tape Street is Cheadle Mill, which dates from 1790s and contains rows of iron columns and roof trusses, an early and good example of industrial architecture.

See chapter 5 for Cheadle's Anglican and Roman Catholic churches.

CHECKLEY

4 miles (6 km) from Cheadle, this village has one of the finest churches in the district, and one that blends work of many periods. The fourteenth-century chancel contains Flemish glass of a century earlier. The font is Norman and the carved stalls date from 1535. In the churchyard are the shafts of three Saxon crosses.

CHEDDLETON

This village by the river Churnet once had a Saxon manor. Beside the thirteenth-century church are the old village stocks, while inside the church there are stained glass windows by William Morris and Ford Madox Brown. A friend of Morris was churchwarden here. Cheddleton Flint Mill and the Cheddleton Railway Centre are described in chapter 7.

CODSALL

Codsall is a charming yet often busy village which lies only a few miles north-west of Wolverhampton. It is referred to in the Domesday Book as part of the township of Oaken. The parish church of St Nicholas has a fine Norman archway and an Early English square tower.

Codsall is famous for its lupins, which are a result of the development here of the Russell lupin, affected by the medicinal springs in the Codsall Wood area.

Just north of Codsall, Pendrell Hall, built in the middle of the nineteenth century, is a mixture of decadent Gothic and Tudor domestic style, standing atop a slope which gives a commanding view on a clear day of the Welsh Marches, Cannock Chase, Wolverhampton and the Black Country. The hall was extensively renovated from around 1910 and is managed by Staffordshire County Council as a residential college.

DARLASTON

In the south-west of what is now the Metropolitan Borough of Walsall, a part of Staffordshire until local government reorganisation in 1974, lies Darlaston. The town's name is probably Anglo-Saxon in origin but little is known of its early history. By the thirteenth century Darlaston is recorded as a small village clustered around the church, on its present site, and the manor house. Present-day street names, like Mill Street and Pinfold Street, reflect those village origins. Mining and metal began to supersede agriculture as Darlaston's trade in the eighteenth century, with the town becoming a world-famous centre for the making of gunlocks.

Today a conservation area has been created to cover some of Darlaston town centre. Buildings of note within this area are 35 King Street (once a private house), the White Lion, numbers 1, 2 and 3 Church Street and St Lawrence's church. Also of note are the Town Hall (1897) and St Joseph's church, built in the shape of a nut to symbolise the town's industrial base.

DENSTONE

Close to Alton and the Churnet valley, Denstone has some fine historic buildings. These include the tavern (1669), Oak Farm

(1701), Lower House (1680) and Manor House (1708). Denstone Hall stands on the site of a house originally built in 1293.

DRAYCOTT-IN-THE-MOORS

South-west of Cheadle and watered by the river Blythe, Draycott-in-the-Moors is a pleasant agricultural village. Its thirteenth-century church contains the Draycott Chapel, with many monuments and effigies to members of the family of that name.

ECCLESHALL

North of Stafford and west of Stone, Eccleshall could be described either as a large village or a small market town. There is a very attractive wide High Street with some charming and individual shops and Georgian houses. Two old inns have arcades built out across the pavement. At one end of the High Street there is a crossroads, and Eccleshall is a meeting place for roads from Newcastle-under-Lyme, Market Drayton, Stone, Stafford and Newport. The other end of the High Street is dominated by the huge parish church, which dates from the thirteenth century. The church is so large because the nearby Eccleshall Castle (what remains is now a private house) was the residence of the Bishops of Lichfield for hundreds of years. No fewer than five former bishops are buried in the church. Near to Eccleshall are Izaak Walton's Cottage and Mill Meece Pumping Station (see chapter 7).

ELLASTONE

Ellastone is typical of the villages in the Weaver Hills which were featured in George Eliot's novel *Adam Bede*. Here the river Dove divides Staffordshire from Derbyshire, and there is an attractive eighteenth-century bridge.

ENDON

Endon lies on the road from Leek to Hanley and is one of the villages where the custom of well dressing still survives. It is thought the custom is based on pagan belief in well worship. The ceremony takes place during the Spring Bank Holiday weekend and has been re-enacted almost every year since its revival in 1845. It includes the coronation of a Well-dressing Queen, who is actually crowned four times — on the Saturday afternoon following a church service, early on Saturday evening and twice on the Monday when the village

fete and fair are held. Morris dancing and a rural competition known as Tossing the Sheaf take place at the same time as the dressing on the Monday. The village centres around St Luke's, a nineteenth-century church with a small seventeenth-century tower.

FARLEY

East of Cheadle and close to Alton Towers, Farley is an attractive village in the Churnet valley. The village's neat stone houses are gathered around the half-timbered early nineteenth-century Farley Hall.

FLASH

High in the Staffordshire Moorlands, Flash, at 1518 feet (463 metres), is reputed to be the highest village in England and was once the centre for counterfeiting money. The counties of Staffordshire, Cheshire and Derbyshire meet at Three Shires Head, and it was relatively easy for the counterfeiters to escape the county sheriff by crossing into another county with their 'Flash' money.

The church is late Victorian Gothic, with a notably elaborate stone pulpit.

GREAT HAYWOOD

Close to the main A51, the old village of Great Haywood has the longest packhorse bridge in England. The sixteenth-century Essex Bridge still has fourteen of its original forty arches, spanning the river Trent.

GRINDON

Grindon lies at the confluence of the rivers Manifold and Hamps, more than 1000 feet (300 metres) above sea level. Picturesque views can be enjoyed of hills, valleys and woods, while moorlands stretch to the west.

Grindon church dates from 1854 and has an unusual octagonal spire and a Norman font from an earlier building on the site.

HEATH HAYES

In the south-eastern part of the Cannock Chase District, Heath Hayes is equidistant from Cannock, Hednesford and the northern edge of Chasewater. Formerly a mining community, Heath Hayes now has other industries. It has extensive new housing, shops, schools and a park. The brick-built church, erected in 1902-3, is quite formal in style but has some originality in its design.

Facing page: *The village cross at Ilam.*

46

HEDNESFORD

Hednesford lies just north-east of Cannock, close to the edges of the Chase. Its oldest building of interest is the Cross Keys Inn, a hostelry of 1746. The Anglesey Hotel, which stands at the end of the main square, was built in 1831 by Edmund Peel of Fazeley as a form of summerhouse. It is designed in a Tudor style with stepped gables.

At Church Hill is the parish church of St Peter, built in 1868 and extended in 1906. The church is Early English in style. Its oldest possession is a silver-gilt medieval chalice thought possibly to be Flemish. The Roman Catholic church of Our Lady of Lourdes is described in chapter 5. On the Rugeley road from the town is the Valley Heritage Centre (see chapter 8).

HOLLINSCLOUGH

On the Staffordshire-Derbyshire border and only 4 miles (6 km) from Buxton, Hollinsclough stands high above the upper Dove valley on gritstone, but against a background of limestone hills. The church and school were built together in 1840, as a single unit. The church, well proportioned and with a gallery, contains fine clear glass and painted texts on its walls.

ILAM

Close to the meeting place of the Dove and Manifold rivers, Ilam is beautiful village in a beautiful setting and with fine views of the peaks that guard this entrance to Dovedale. Ilam's natural beauty is said to have suggested the idea of the Happy Valley to Rasselas and also to have provided the setting for Congreve's *The Old Bachelor*. In the midst of woods and gardens are the church, hall and park (see chapter 2) and the village cross, which much resembles one of the Eleanor crosses.

Ilam church is described in chapter 5.

IPSTONES

One of the largest villages in the Staffordshire Moorlands, Ipstones is almost wholly built of stone and its quaint and narrow lanes are set in superb country. A lively village, Ipstones has several old houses of note, including the eighteenth-century ashlar-built house called The Swagger and Muss Lee Hall of 1640. The church is of the late eighteenth century, with a screen that fills the entire chancel arch and has above it a painting of

Christ in Glory.

The village is the centre of one of Staffordshire's most recent and most successful industries — farm holidays, a group of local farmers having formed a co-operative to promote the idea, and at Ipstones Edge is Moorlands Farm Park of British Rare Breeds and Domestic Animals (see chapter 8).

KEELE

Keele is a small village 2 miles (3 km) west of Newcastle-under-Lyme. The University of Keele stands in a beautiful 650 acre (263 ha) country estate, formerly the home of the Sneyd family, who owned extensive areas of north Staffordshire around 1900. Keele was the first of the post-war universities. Founded in 1949, it adopted an original approach to university education, stemming from the thinking of its first Principal, Lord Lindsay. It is now the largest and one of the most attractive of Britain's campuses. The university has one of the highest proportions in Britain — some 85 per cent — of students and staff in residence. The university also hosts a growing conference trade.

The village of Keele has a shop and post office, a public house called the Sneyd Arms, a parish church and a village hall.

KIDSGROVE

Kidsgrove is a town which has developed around the site of an old north Staffordshire mining community. It is a part of the Borough of Newcastle but retains its own town council. Until the eighteenth century the land on which Kidsgrove stands today consisted of parkland with extensively wooded areas, and such cottages as did exist then could not have been said to have constituted a village, so spread-out were they.

The development of the pottery industry in nearby Stoke-on-Trent in the early eighteenth century led to demand for improved transport and brought the canal and later the railway to the Kidsgrove area. The canal engineer James Brindley constructed the remarkable Harecastle Tunnel under the ridge at Kidsgrove (see chapter 9) and settlements began to grow up around the canal wharves. Exploitation of the area for iron and then coal boosted the local population and the nineteenth-century town began to take shape. Many of the small cottages were built at this time, as were Clough Hall, a substantial country house now demolished, several farmhouses, shops and a market.

St Thomas's church was built in 1837, with a slightly later chancel, to designs by Sir George Gilbert Scott.

Nearby **Talke** was incorporated into Kidsgrove in the 1930s and has a stone cross dated 1253 which is thought to have stood on the site of a market. Butt Lane was the birthplace of the designer of the Spitfire aircraft, Reginald Mitchell. St Martin's church in Talke was erected in 1794 on the site of a much earlier church whose possessions are recorded as being surrendered to royal commissioners in 1553.

At **Newchapel**, nearby, is St James's church, built in 1880 as a memorial to James Brindley, whose remains are interred here.

KING'S BROMLEY

This is one of Staffordshire's oldest villages, once the home of Leofric, the Saxon Earl of Mercia, and his wife, Lady Godiva. Leofric died here. King's Bromley was a crown property for many years after the Norman conquest and it had other royal connections in the twelfth century, when Henry I stayed here and used the forests for hunting, and in the seventeenth century, when Charles II was helped to escape by the Lane family, who lived locally.

KINVER

The village of Kinver lies in the extreme south of Staffordshire, close to its boundary with Hereford and Worcester. Traces of an ancient British camp have been found at Kinver Edge. The parish was described as 'Chenevare' in the Domesday Book and was once, like so much of Staffordshire, royal hunting forest land. It was also, because of its closeness to the river Stour, a centre for trading.

Kinver's High Street has some pleasant houses and shops of the seventeenth and eighteenth centuries, with a church thought to date from the fourteenth or fifteenth century.

The Rock Houses at Kinver are dwellings which have been hewn from the soft Triassic sandstone outcrops of Kinver Edge since the iron age (see chapter 2). By the nineteenth century the interiors of the rock houses were comparable with ordinary homes built of brick, with natural cavities in the rock having been enlarged into rooms with doorways, windows and masonry chimneys. Cupboards

Market Street, Lichfield.

and storage areas were cut into the walls of each of the houses just as in an ordinary home and the last of the rock houses was not vacated by its residents until the 1960s.

KNYPERSLEY

Knypersley, near Biddulph, is particularly noted for its church. St John's was built in 1851 at the expense of James Bateman of Biddulph Grange, who also paid for the huge neo-Jacobean parsonage and the school. His own house was noted for its gardens, which were started in the 1850s and became a superb example of a high Victorian garden (see chapter 6). The house was rebuilt in 1876 for his son.

LEEK

Market day Wednesday.

Set in beautiful countryside of hills, moors and dales, Leek is frequently described as the 'Queen of the Staffordshire Moorlands'. Leek is an important market town serving a large rural area of north Staffordshire. It is also an industrial town renowned for the manufacture of silk products and dyes. Although these have been largely superseded by modern synthetics, the character of the industry has been retained through the continued use of the old mill buildings. The essential character of Leek, however, remains that of a pleasant rural town with a weekly cattle and open-air market.

The town centre is well worth walking around, with its good range of shops including many selling antiques. There are many fine buildings too, including the parish church of St Edward the Confessor, built in 1297 (see chapter 5), and the Roebuck Inn, in Derby Street, dated 1627. Most of the town's finest buildings, however, date from the nineteenth century and many are the work of the Sugdens, two worthy local architects. On the edge of the town centre is Brough Park with its informal walks and flower gardens, but nowhere in Leek is it possible to forget the surrounding countryside as there are glimpses of it even from the town centre.

Brindley Mill and the Leek Art Gallery are described in chapter 7.

LICHFIELD

Market days Friday and Saturday.

Lichfield, the old capital of Staffordshire and the birthplace of Samuel Johnson, is rich in memories of such other notabilities as Erasmus Darwin, Garrick and Addison. These characters made the city a classic centre of

49

the arts and learning not only in Johnson's age but in the generations before and after.

Lichfield's history begins with visitors who came on pilgrimage to the tomb of St Chad. A church was dedicated to St Chad and gradually over the centuries this developed into a cathedral (see chapter 5). Perhaps the finest feature of Lichfield Cathedral is the surrounding close with its gravelled walks and fine buildings like the Deanery and the Bishop's Palace. Tucked away in the corner is Vicars' Close, with sixteenth-century timbered houses.

For many hundreds of years the Cathedral Close and the city were separated by wide swamps (known locally as the Moggs), which could only be crossed by ferryboat or narrow causeway. Today the swamps are the Stowe and Minster Pools, pleasant expanses of water surrounded by fields and gardens, which provide facilities for anglers and yachtsmen, as well as a home for wildfowl.

The medieval pattern of Lichfield's streets is still evident today, but the golden age of the city and its buildings was the eighteenth century. Two of the most attractive Georgian houses can be seen around Stowe Pool. Lichfield's reputation as the home or birthplace of many eminent men and women in the eighteenth century gave the city the name of the 'Athens of the Midlands'. The house of David Garrick, the famous actor, no longer stands but the birthplace of his friend, Dr Johnson, in Breadmarket Street, is now a museum to his life and work (see chapter 7). A large nineteenth-century statue stands in the Market Place opposite Johnson's birthplace, as does a charming, more recent statue of Johnson's friend and biographer, James Boswell. A more grim relic of those times is the city dungeons, under the Victorian Gothic guildhall in Bore Street.

Since at least the seventeenth century Lichfield has been famous for beer and public houses. Many of these still remain and elsewhere in the city the narrow streets and old buildings have encouraged the establishment of several specialist shops. And after exploring the cathedral, the museums and the shops, there is Beacon Park, an excellent recreation area and picnic place. Nearby at Wall can be seen the remains of the Roman fort of Letocetum (see chapter 3).

The annual Lichfield Festival, held each summer, provides a wealth of artistic performances to suit a variety of tastes, often featuring performers of international standing.

See chapter 5 for St Mary's and St Michael's churches and chapter 7 for museums and art galleries.

LITTLE WYRLEY

Little Wyrley is near Norton Canes, in the southerly part of the Cannock Chase District, to the south of Watling Street. It is largely open country and farmland. Wyrley Common is a notable feature and at the hamlet of Little Wyrley itself is the oldest house in the area, Little Wyrley Hall. The oldest part of this house was timber-framed and dates from the sixteenth century. In 1660 a brick-faced wing was added and other rooms followed in 1691, thus hiding the original core of the building. The hall, which is not open to view, contains some fine seventeenth-century panelling, very ornate early door furniture and a beautiful staircase.

LONGNOR

This small town near Staffordshire's northern boundary stands on the neck of land between the Manifold and the Dove, in the heart of the Staffordshire Moorlands. Its white stone houses and little market hall cluster around the green. The hall, a delightful little building, dates from 1873. The church of 1780 is a large and striking building with, unusually, two tiers of windows on each side of the nave, the upper tier specially built to light side galleries that are no longer there. The font is Norman and survives from an earlier church on this site.

LONGSDON

A village on the Leek to Hanley road, Longsdon is the centre of an extensive and wooded parish that extends to the Churnet and includes the high land of Ladderedge as well as the hamlet of Horse Bridge. Longsdon's church is dedicated to St Chad and was built in 1905. The church has a splendid west tower capped by a broach spire and the fine stained glass in the east window is by Comper.

MADELEY

Situated on a packhorse route from Newcastle-under-Lyme, Madeley's name comes from the Anglo-Saxon *maden lieg*, which means 'clearing in the woods'.

The centre of Madeley is designated a con-

Quoinians Lane, Lichfield.

servation area. Its central feature is the Pool, which was formed by damming the river Lea to provide water power for the corn mill built at its northern end. The grandest building is the Old Hall, a sixteenth-century timber-framed house. Its western elevation carries the inscription, 'Walk Knave. Waht's lookest at'. It is thought that this inscription was added in 1647 so that local Roundheads would not suspect the owners of Royalist sympathies.

MARCHINGTON

With its seventeenth-century hall and eighteenth-century church, Marchington has a distinctive and historic flavour. Much of the village is in a conservation area and of particular interest are the seventeenth-century timber-framed St Anne's Lodge and the High Street.

Marchington Woodlands is a country area in which is set a fine example of a preserved

private dwelling of 1600, Woodruffs, which still bears the names of the original family scratched on to the kitchen windowpanes.

NEWCASTLE-UNDER-LYME
Market days Monday, Friday and Saturday.

Newcastle lies in north-west Staffordshire on the watershed between the Trent and the Cheshire Plain. The town's history owes much to its strategic position at the junction of routes from the north-west to the Midlands and south. The borough is thought to have received its first charter from Henry II in 1173 and for several centuries the town was the largest in north Staffordshire. Its castle was 'new' in relation to the Roman fort or an unrecorded medieval castle at Chesterton and occupied a mound protected by an artificial lake, between Pooldam and Rotterdam on the Lyme Brook.

The town soon became the main route and

51

The Guildhall, Newcastle-under-Lyme.

market centre in north Staffordshire. A new era of road building began in the seventeenth century, followed in the eighteenth and nineteenth centuries by canal and railway construction. Together with the growth of coal mining, these developments emphasised the importance of the area as a route centre and brought larger-scale industries than the crafts which had existed previously. In this period of growth the nearby Pottery towns grew more rapidly but, as Newcastle-under-Lyme was situated to the smoke-free south-west and was less heavily industrialised, it became, and still remains, a desirable residential area.

Today the town has a busy market, which dates back eight hundred years, and attractive shopping facilities. The town centre is designated a conservation area and many listed buildings carry an identification plaque.

Two town trails have been established by

Newcastle Borough Council, taking in buildings of interest. Both these walks begin in Nelson Place. The first walk follows Queen Street, visiting St George's church (1828) and Mayer House, built in 1785 and the former home of a famous veterinary family. Houses in Brampton Park include two which have become the museum and the arts centre. King Street has some fine Georgian houses, while the large, white nineteenth-century building in Marsh Parade was the town's first silk mill. Holy Trinity Roman Catholic church was built in 1834 with local materials, Staffordshire blue brick and cast iron. The old barracks, built in 1855 for the local militia or volunteer force, is now a centre for craft industries.

A second town trail takes in the attractive Merrial Street, where there are fine views, then moves on to St Giles's church. The base of its tower dates from the thirteenth century but a classical brick church replaced the medieval one in 1720, before it was rebuilt again in the original style by George Gilbert Scott in the 1870s. Pooldam is a reminder of the defensive pool of the twelfth-century castle from which the town takes its name. High Street has some interesting buildings, notably the Park Shop, once the Golden Bell Inn, a timber-framed building of about 1600. The wide High Street and the market area reflect the medieval need for open space and with the narrow lanes and alleys they form a grid plan typical of a medieval town.

The Guildhall (1713) replaced an earlier timber building and beside it is the base of a medieval market cross. Through narrow Cheapside is the Ironmarket, so named because of the flourishing local iron trade, Nelson Place was reclaimed from marshland in 1782 and laid out as a central open space with several short streets radiating from it.

The Newcastle Borough Museum and Hobbergate Art Gallery are described in chapter 7.

NORTON CANES

South of Heath Hayes and extending to Watling Street is Norton Canes, which, with Norton East, forms an extensive industrial and residential area on the west side of Chasewater. Formerly a coal-mining area, it now lies close to the pleasure park of Chasewater itself. Norton Canes has developed considerably in post-war years. At the western end of the older part of the village is the church of St James, a building first erected in 1832 and then rebuilt in 1888. The west tower has large pinnacles, the main style of the building being Perpendicular.

OAKAMOOR

Oakamoor was once an industrial centre where copper was produced but it is now a small residential village situated amongst superb scenery in one of the steepest and most heavily wooded parts of the Churnet valley (see chapter 2). The parish church dates from 1832 and is built on such a steep slope that it has a lower church or hall below the high-level church above. Nearby is the Memorial Chapel, a nonconformist place of worship built in 1878 by members of the Bolton family, who owned and operated the copper works at that time.

ONECOTE

East of Leek, this is a high moorland parish watered by the river Hamps, and the village is situated at the point where this river is bridged by the Buxton to Ipstones road. The castellated parish church tower dates from the eighteenth century and inside the church is a pulpit with tester of the same period. Remains of former copper mines can be found throughout the locality.

PENKRIDGE
Market days Wednesday and Saturday.

Between Stafford and Wolverhampton, and skirted both by the M6 motorway and a main railway line, Penkridge is one of Staffordshire's larger commuter villages. Yet Penkridge has a pleasant, lively heart, some interesting buildings, and a particularly good outdoor market.

A market in Penkridge can be traced to the granting of a market charter by King Henry III in 1244. Queen Elizabeth I is reported to have visited the White Hart Inn and other ancient features include the church of St Michael and All Angels, the stocks and jail at the constable's house – Cruck Cottage, Bellbrook – the Old Deanery Farm House and Church Cottage.

The parish church dominates the centre of Penkridge and was one of six collegiate churches in Staffordshire before the Reformation. Built of local red sandstone, the church has some fine old woodwork in the choir stalls and slabs, tombs and monuments with inscriptions of particular interest to those studying the history of local families.

PYE GREEN

Pye Green, a residential area near Hednesford, is dominated by the Telecom Tower. Built in 1970, this stark and futuristic-looking tower is 258 feet (79 metres) high and, as it stands on land that is 775 feet (236 metres) above sea level, it is the most conspicuous feature of this part of Staffordshire, visible from many miles away.

ROCESTER

There had already been a settlement at Rocester for between two and three thousand years when the Romans settled there on the route between Derby and Chesterton (see chapter 3). Archaeological surveys by air have indicated prehistoric remains and a pot found by archaeologists has been dated to 2000 BC. There are still visible traces of the original Roman camp, of an Augustinian abbey and of the much later Tutbury Mill, which owes its origins to Richard Arkwright.

The churchyard of St Michael's contains the shaft of a Saxon cross, while Rocester today is home of the international company J. C. Bamford, whose striking factory premises are set in superbly landscaped lakes and parkland.

ROLLESTON

Though the village is sometimes known as Rolleston-on-Dove, it is the Alder Brook, flowing through the centre of the village, which gives a distinctive and unusual identity to this place. Much expanded in modern times, Rolleston was a settlement long ago, with the first written record of the village appearing in AD 942. St Mary's parish church dates from the twelfth century and contains interesting monuments to local families as well as being a local landmark.

RUGELEY
Market days Tuesday, Thursday, Friday and Saturday.

Situated alongside the river Trent and on the borders of Cannock Chase, Rugeley is an excellent centre for exploring the surrounding area. The town has an intimate character, having retained its medieval street layout despite serious fires in 1649 and 1708. Now designated a conservation area, Rugeley has many attractive buildings, including some on Horsefair and in Market Place dating from the seventeenth and eighteenth centuries. The slender clock tower which overlooks Market

Shenstone.

Place was built in 1879 and formed part of the old indoor market, now replaced by a fine market hall on the site of the old Town Mill. A walk down Market Street leads to Rugeley's oldest building, the former parish church of St Augustine, of which the tower dating from the thirteenth and fourteenth centuries, chancel and north chapel still remain (see chapter 5). Nearby passes the Trent and Mersey Canal, which brought prosperity to the town following its completion in 1777. Shopping is a pleasure in the town's traffic-free streets.

SHENSTONE

The village of Shenstone, about 5 miles (8 km) south of Lichfield, and with a population of nearly seven thousand, dates back to before the Norman conquest. It sits on a hillside with two church towers at the top and is surrounded by woods. The older buildings date from the seventeenth to the nineteenth century.

STAFFORD

Market days Tuesday, Friday and Saturday.

The county town since the eleventh century, Stafford today has a population of approximately 56,000 people. Stafford is famous for its connections with Izaak Walton, the author of *The Compleat Angler*, Josiah Wedgwood, the potter, and the playwright

Sheridan, who was also Stafford's Member of Parliament for twenty-six years. Charles Dickens and George Borrow both stayed at the Elizabethan Swan Hotel in the centre of the town.

The present town centre is the site of the original town, which was an island in the middle of marshes on an ancient trackway. The name Stafford is of Saxon origin and means 'a ford at a landing place' (*staith-ford*). Ethelfleda, daughter of Alfred the Great and widow of Ethelred, Earl of Mercia, fortified the settlement in AD 913 against the Danes. The town was probably a trading centre from early times and there was a royal mint here from the reign of Athelstan (924-39) until that of Henry II (1154-89). In 1206 King John granted the town a charter, recognising its borough status.

The street pattern of the town has not changed greatly over the centuries. Originally the streets were full of timber-framed buildings but most of these have disappeared, the victims of either fire or redevelopment. One outstanding building of historic interest which has survived is the Ancient High House of the Tudor period in Greengate Street (see chapter 7).

A lively and bustling town, Stafford has maintained much of its historic charm alongside busy shops, a thriving market and industries that include engineering, shoemaking, computers and industrial equipment.

A Stafford town trail has been designed by the borough council. It starts at Eastgate, at the end of Eastgate Street, where lie the remains of the last of the town's four gates. Elizabeth I entered here on her visit in 1575. The road beyond crosses marshy ground, the site of medieval fishponds.

The William Salt Library, now in Eastgate Street, was first housed in Old Bank House, Market Square. It was founded in 1872 for the collection of documents, books and pictures begun by William Salt, a banker and antiquarian (see chapter 7).

Pitcher Bank is a name derived from a street market selling crockery on the site before 1881. Livestock was sold in other streets round the Market Square. Izaak Walton, author of *The Compleat Angler*, is said to have been born in a house on the south side of the

The Ancient High House, Stafford.

street and there is a memorial bust to him in St Mary's church, where he was baptised in 1593.

County Buildings in Martin Street was designed by Henry Hare, a London architect who also designed Oxford Town Hall. Opened in 1895 for the new county council, it was described by Pevsner as 'baroque with gusto'.

The earliest reference to Market Square, in respect of a riot, is 1230. A shire hall was built there in 1587. The square was cleared of stalls in 1881 when the present market hall was extended. The present Shire Hall, to the east of the old one, was built in 1798 by John Harvey, pupil of Samuel Wyatt, as a court house and office for the clerk of the peace and the mayor.

St Chad's church has Norman work found in 1854 under brick and plaster covering. The nave arcading, chancel arch and chancel are original. The church was restored and enlarged by Sir George Gilbert Scott in 1874-5.

The Post Office is the town house of about 1740 of the Chetwynds of Ingestre. It was the home of William Horton (1750-1832), founder of the town's boot and shoe industry and friend of Richard Brinsley Sheridan, the playwright and Member of Parliament for Stafford, who stayed at the house.

Green Bridge was the site of a ford. The earliest record of a bridge was in 1285. For St Mary's church see chapter 5.

The Ancient High House is said to be the largest timber-framed town house in England. It was built of local oak in 1595 by John Dorrington. Charles I stopped there and, from the back garden, Prince Rupert used the weathercock of St Mary's church for a target. It served as a prison for Royalists during the Civil War.

The Swan Hotel in Greengate Street was converted from a seventeenth-century town house to form the town's most important coaching inn. The arched entrance may still be seen, although the passage floor has been raised above street level by steps. It was associated with George Borrow, author of *Romany Rye*, and with Charles Dickens.

Town Mill was probably the site of a watermill since as early as 1086. The last mill was demolished in 1957, but the waterwheels have been preserved on the site.

Sir Martin Noel's Almshouses were built about 1660 by Sir Martin for six poor men and six poor women of the town. He was a native of Stafford, supported Cromwell and was a Member of Parliament. He died of the plague in London in 1665. The chapel contains glass from Castle Church.

Tenterbanks was the site where medieval weavers stretched their cloth to dry on tenterhooks.

Broad Eye mill was built as a windmill in 1796 of stones from the Elizabethan shire hall. It bears the initials of John Wright, whose family was still operating it in 1818. By 1847 it was steam-driven and it remained in use until the 1880s. It stands on the possible site of a castle built by William the Conqueror to hold the town in subjection. The adjoining river bridge was the main western entrance of the town in ancient times.

Stafford's museums are described in chapter 7 and the castle in chapter 4.

STOKE-ON-TRENT

Stoke-on-Trent, a city of about 36 square miles (93 sq km), was formed by the federation, in 1910, of the six towns of Tunstall, Burslem, Fenton, Longton, Stoke and Hanley. Known world-wide as 'The Potteries', the city owes its existence to the development there of the ceramics industry, which still flourishes. Other industries, notably coal mining, engineering, chemicals and rubber, provide a solid commercial base for the area.

The city of Stoke-on-Trent offers the visitor the opportunity to explore the nation's industrial heritage and an excellent base from which to venture into some of England's finest countryside. Within an hour's drive is the Peak District National Park, a beautiful area of rocky hills, stone walls and windy ridges. The city itself is a product of the industrial revolution, with an economy based on 'pits and pots'; today it offers fascinating living museums which enable the visitor to witness the past at work. The city has been transformed in recent years, particularly through land reclamation schemes, which constitute some of the most dramatic city improvements in Britain. These include the creation of a forest park on the edge of Hanley centre and a country park at Park Hall with its imaginative landscape and spectacular views over the city to the Pennines (see chapter 2). A system of 'Greenways' has been opened up for pedestrians and horse riders, using abandoned railway lines, and the city's canals provide a system of 'Blueways' along which to explore.

When Stoke-on-Trent was selected as the site of the 1986 National Garden Festival, nearly 200 acres (81 ha) of the former Shelton Steelworks site were reclaimed as attractive industrial and park land.

By 1880 the six independent towns of the Potteries had grown in population, density, complexity and interdependence. Their principal mutual concerns were the protection of life and property, through good policing, the improvement of roads and lighting. In 1839 Acts of Parliament provided a Potteries stipendiary magistrate and an effective police force. Local patriotism, sometimes strident opposition and the improving status of each of the six towns continually delayed amalgamation but by 1888 their mutual problems of roads, sewage, water, housing and gas supplies, together with increased pressure from central government and the county, finally forced the six towns to combine.

Burslem
Market day Saturday.

Burslem has been called the mother town of the Potteries, although it was still a village of fewer than seventy houses in 1680. However, mining and pottery making had been in progress since as early as the fourteenth century and Royal Doulton is still there (see chapter 8). Nonetheless, Burslem's rural character was retained until its development as a market town began after 1761. Rapid expansion during the nineteenth century provided good housing for the town's workers.

Burslem has two town halls. The Old Town Hall, now the Burslem Leisure Centre, stands in the middle of the Market Place and is surmounted by the angel immortalised by Arnold Bennett, the famous novelist of the Five Towns. At the beginning of the twentieth century Bennett, through novels such as *The Old Wives' Tale* and *Clayhanger*, ably interpreted the social and commercial life of the Staffordshire Potteries. Burslem's historic town centre appears in his novels, thinly disguised, as 'Bursley'.

Fenton
Market day Thursday.

Fenton today is made up of Fenton Culvert and Fenton Vivian and is the largest of the six towns in area. By 1700 coal and iron were being produced here and iron was being smelted by 1840. Ten years later pottery production had increased quite dramatically, but housing and sanitation were bad, with piped water only just becoming available. Fenton's town hall is in Albert Square and is now used as the city's magistrates court. This former coal-mining village now has other industries as well as the third largest park in the city. Fenton is the home of Coalport bone china and the Heron Cross Pottery (see chapter 8).

Hanley
Market days Wednesday, Friday and Saturday.

Hanley was the scene of coal mining by 1297 and pottery production was being carried on by 1700. By the middle of the nineteenth century it was the largest of the six towns. Iron from its mines was being smelted by this time, and in 1864 forges and mills were added. Today, Hanley is the principal shopping and commercial centre of the city. Here are the department stores, specialist shops, offices and entertainment and recrea-

St Peter's church, Stoke-on-Trent.

tion facilities. The Stoke-on-Trent City Museum and Art Gallery (see chapter 7) includes one of the largest and most important collections of English pottery and porcelain. Orchestral concerts and other entertainments are held at the Victoria Hall.

Longton
Market days Monday to Saturday.

Longton in 1666 was a hamlet of twelve houses and was known then as Lane End. It was not until 1848 that the name Longton was adopted, when the place had become a sprawling, irregularly built market town, its development accelerated by the expansion of mining, ironworking, pottery manufacture, tilemaking and brewing. Longton's main streets converge on the Market Place, with the town hall in the centre. Redevelopment of the central area has produced a strikingly busy shopping centre, with a pedestrian shopping precinct, new bus station and central car park. Here too is the famous Gladstone Pottery Museum (see chapter 7) and the factories of John Beswick and Royal Grafton China (see chapter 8).

Stoke
Market days Wednesday and Friday.

Stoke in the middle ages had little more than a parish church, and Penkhull was the main centre of population. The development of Stoke as a town began in the mid eighteenth century, with the growth of the pottery industry in north Staffordshire and the coming of turnpike roads, canals and later the railway. In 1851 Stoke was described as 'picturesque', although fever was a serious problem in the town due to bad drainage.

Stoke itself is the centre of local government for the city of Stoke-on-Trent and the town hall in Glebe Street is one of the finest buildings in north Staffordshire. St Peter's church, also in Glebe Street, has monuments to the eminent potters of the eighteenth and nineteenth centuries: Josiah Wedgwood, Josiah Spode (father and son) and William Adams. Fine new buildings in this part of the city include the North Staffordshire Polytechnic. Winton Square, which incorporated both the main railway station and the North Stafford Hotel, is of great architectural interest and contains a splendid statue of Josiah Wedgwood.

In Stoke are the factories of Minton and Spode (see chapter 8).

The Dog and Partridge Hotel, Tutbury.

Tunstall

Tunstall's early history is also associated with the production of coal and iron, yet in 1811 there were only 335 inhabited houses there. But by 1817 the town was producing high-quality blue tiles and had its own town hall. There was also a market, and a building society had erected forty terraced houses. From then on Tunstall grew steadily, from village to market and industrial town, with potteries, collieries, ironstone mines and brick and tile works. The Chatterley Whitfield Mining Museum (see chapter 7) is nearby.

Town trails

The best way of exploring the whole of the city of Stoke-on-Trent is to follow one of the town trails, promoted by the city council's tourist office, which introduce the characteristic features of the Potteries landscape, through canals, historic industrial buildings and much more.

STONE

Market day Tuesday.

Stone, midway between Stafford and Stoke-on-Trent, is an attractive shopping and residential town. Stone became a market town in 1251 when Henry III granted the monks a

Tuesday market with a three-day fair in July. It also derived importance from the coaching trade and as many as thirty-eight coaches a day used to pull up at the Crown Hotel in the centre of the town. With the coming of the railways in the nineteenth century the town lost its flow of passing travellers.

The Trent and Mersey Canal played a large part in the town's early economic development and even today it still brings work to Stone through the building of holiday canal cruisers and a growing tourist trade.

See chapter 5 for the church.

TAMWORTH

Market days Tuesday and Saturday.

Tamworth is situated in the south-east corner of Staffordshire. Originally an important town in the Saxon kingdom of Mercia, Tamworth is today a commercial centre for the surrounding rural area, and a modern industrial and residential borough, having become an overspill town for Birmingham in recent years. Yet Tamworth is a town of historic atmosphere, with several ancient buildings surviving, including the well preserved remains of its Norman castle, in which is housed an excellent museum.

The earliest reference to the town is in a

58

charter signed by Offa, king of Mercia, on St Stephen's Day, AD 781. In 1967 remains of a timber stockade were found which was built by Aethelflaed, daughter of Alfred the Great, during her successful war against the Danes about 913. Tamworth prospered during this period and about 926 a mint was established.

Following the Norman Conquest the present castle (see chapter 4) was built by Robert de Marmion, Lord of Fontenaye and Royal Champion. Part of the castle houses a local history museum.

Queen Elizabeth I granted a Charter of Incorporation to the town in 1560 and during the latter part of the sixteenth century additional privileges were given. Tamworth's finest example of Elizabethan architecture is the Moat House, situated off Lichfield Road.

Tamworth has had two illustrious Members of Parliament: Sir Robert Peel, exponent of free trade, founder of the police force and prime minister; and Thomas Guy, who founded Guy's Hospital, London. Tamworth's town hall was built in 1700 by Thomas Guy and standing in front of the building is a statue of Sir Robert Peel.

See chapter 5 for St Editha's church.

TEAN

Tean, a village south of Cheadle, is dominated by tall nineteenth-century tape mills. But there are also some attractive houses and cottages of the seventeenth and eighteenth centuries and an early nineteenth-century Gothic church.

TUTBURY

Tutbury is a small market town, dating from the eleventh century, with a ruined castle (see chapter 4). The town's history dates back to Anglo-Saxon times, being close to the geographical centre of the old kingdom of Mercia and its capital at Repton (Derbyshire). The ancient craft of glassmaking thrives at Tutbury, and craftsmen can be seen at work making and decorating glassware. Their products are on sale in the town (see chapter 8). The sixteenth-century Dog and Partridge Hotel in the High Street is one of Tutbury's oldest buildings, having once been a busy coaching inn.

UTTOXETER
Market day Wednesday and Saturday.

The town of Uttoxeter is busiest on Wednesday, when the traditional livestock and street market is held. Disastrous fires in 1596 and 1672 destroyed much of the town's historic architecture, although several old timbered buildings have survived in the market place. The Heritage Centre in Carter Street is in restored seventeenth-century cottages (see chapter 8).

The town is known for its association with Dr Samuel Johnson, who, as a boy, refused to attend his father's bookstall in the market place. When aged about seventy, he returned to the market place and stood bareheaded in the rain as an act of penance and this is commemorated by a plaque near to the place where his father's stall stood.

Uttoxeter also possesses one of the five municipally owned racecourses in Britain and there are several National Hunt meetings there in the year.

WALSALL
Market days Monday, Tuesday, Friday and Saturday.

Walsall almost certainly existed in Anglo-Saxon times, probably even before then, although the town was not mentioned in the Domesday Book of 1086. Originally called *Walhs Halh*, which means a sheltered place belonging to a Welshman or Welshmen, the town was given to the church of Wolverhampton in 996. During the reign of Edward the Confessor, Walsall was a royal manor, but in 1159 the town was given by King Henry II to Herbert Ruffus, whose family remained lords of the manor for more than two hundred years. Walsall's market was established by a royal charter, known as the Ruffus Charter, in 1219, and it is this charter which is the first evidence of the existence of the Borough of Walsall.

Walsall came to be associated with metal industries from an early date, having abundant resources of coal, iron ore and limestone. The leather trade, for which the town is still famous, had its beginnings alongside the saddlers' ironmongery business and by the nineteenth century leather was Walsall's predominant industry. Every saddle used in the British army during the First World War was said to have been produced in Walsall.

Walsall was one of Staffordshire's largest towns until the reorganisation of local government incorporated the town into the West Midlands metropolitan county in 1974. However, perhaps more than any of the other towns which that reorganisation removed from

CHAPTER 10

Staffordshire, the people of Walsall still tend to regard themselves and their town as being in Staffordshire. The town has two notable conservation areas. The Church Hill conservation area includes St Matthew's church (see chapter 5), George Street, Lower Hall Lane, Goodall Street and Shannon's Factory; and the Town Centre conservation area takes in Bradford Street, Bridge Street, Lichfield Street and Darwall Street. This area has several interesting Victorian buildings and frontages, notably Taylor's Music Shop, which is a remarkable four-storey building in Italian Renaissance style, with some ornate decoration depicting biblical figures, great composers and goddesses. Other notable features of the town include a lively street market and museums and galleries housing distinguished and valuable collections (see chapter 7).

WARSLOW

Warslow village, east of Leek, is a high moorland community that centres around a church built in 1820 and noted for the fine Pre-Raphaelite glass in the chancel windows. The village has many stone houses and a typical Peak District character.

WATERHOUSES

By the banks of the river Hamps is Waterhouses, a straggling village which stands close to the point where the river disappears underground before joining the Manifold. The oldest building is the mid-Georgian Lee House. See chapter 8 for Brooklyn Farm and Craft Workshop.

WEDNESBURY

Market days Friday and Saturday; early closing Thursday.

Wednesbury, now in the Metropolitan Borough of Sandwell, was a Staffordshire town until 1974. In Anglo-Saxon times it was an important fort for Mercia. For hundreds of years Wednesbury was a farming community but when coal was discovered there it began to develop into the industrial town it is today. Notable features are the Art Gallery and Museum in Holyhead Road (see chapter 7) and the conservation area which centres around the market.

WEST BROMWICH

Market days Monday, Thursday, Friday, Saturday; early closing Wednesday.

A part of Staffordshire until 1974, West Bromwich is now the administrative centre of the Metropolitan Borough of Sandwell. West Bromwich in Domesday Book times was agricultural in nature and remained so, and largely self-sufficient, until in the seventeenth century some of its men began to work in the mines as nearby Wednesbury developed as a coal town. The discovery of coal and the position of West Bromwich as a centre of communications contributed to the town's growth as a base for small metal industries such as gunmaking and the manufacture of nails.

Notable buildings include Oak House (see chapter 6), the medieval Manor House and the nineteenth-century town hall with its magnificent organ.

WETTON

On the west side of the deep and beautiful Manifold valley is Wetton, a compact stone village close to Wetton Hill and only a mile across the moors from Alstonefield. All around is the beautiful country of the Staffordshire Moorlands. Nearby is Thor's Cavern, a vast cave that extends for over 100 feet (30 metres) into the rock. Wetton church was rebuilt in 1820 but it retains its fourteenth-century tower with its unusual outside stair turret up to the belfry.

WHITTINGTON

Whittington is the home of the Staffordshire Regiment (the Prince of Wales's) and houses a museum dedicated to the history of the regiment (see chapter 7 under Lichfield). Open land here, just east of Lichfield, was called Whittington Heath. Formerly used as a racecourse, it is now a golf course. The handsome Elizabethan manor house called Whittington Old Hall was once the home of Pagents and Babingtons, who were friends of Mary, Queen of Scots.

WILLENHALL

Market days Wednesday, Friday and Saturday.

Willenhall is another of those towns which were transferred from Staffordshire to West Midlands metropolitan county under the local government reorganisation in 1974.

The name Willenhall is Anglo-Saxon and probably means 'Willa's hall'. It was King Aethelred who first put the town into the history books by signing a charter in 733.

During the reign of Queen Elizabeth I the town was granted the exclusive right to manufacture locks for the state. Today Willenhall produces around 90 per cent of all locks made in the United Kingdom. It was the discovery of coal and iron in the area in the seventeenth century which enabled the industry to become firmly established. Willenhall was known as 'Humpshire' because so many local people had deformed backs caused by being hunched over their lockmaking benches. Today the town has a fascinating Lock Museum and a museum about the town (see chapter 7).

Willenhall's market is the centrepiece of a splendid conservation area resurfaced with blue brick pavements and cast iron kerbing, restoring it to its nineteenth-century splendour.

WOLVERHAMPTON

Wolverhampton is situated on the edge of what has become known as the Black Country, that concentration of industrial areas which has been and still is so important to the economy of the West Midlands region. Wolverhampton was in Staffordshire until the re-organisation of local government in 1974, when it became a metropolitan borough within the metropolitan county of the West Midlands. It is often referred to as the place where agriculture and industry meet.

Although evidence unearthed in the form of a sandstone axe and bronze palstave suggests that an early settlement existed as far back as 1200 BC it was during the Saxon era that the town was first recorded as a community. In 985 the first known charter for Wolverhampton was granted by King Aethelred II (Aethelred the Unready) to a local woman, Lady Wulfruna. The king gave her land at a place called Heantun, meaning 'high town', for her to enjoy during her lifetime, but with freedom to grant the land to others. In 944 Lady Wulfruna gave this land to the monastery of St Mary, which stood where the imposing St Peter's church stands today. Soon afterwards, the name 'Wulfrun Heantun' first appeared, the origin of the present name of Wolverhampton.

Later on, in the thirteenth century, the town was granted a market charter by Henry III, with one of the main commodities traded being wool. It is claimed that Wolverhampton was a major contributor to England's wool exports during this period and the trade of those times is recorded in the names of some of today's streets, such as Farmers Fold, Woolpack Alley and Mitre Fold.

With the discovery of coal and iron, Wolverhampton turned to the working of metals, which was fundamental to the town's future prosperity and development. The town became famous for lockmaking and the manufacture of buckles, metal toys and general hardware, while Bilston became especially renowned as an important enamelling centre. The achievements of those times are brought to life today in Wolverhampton's Art Gallery and Museum, Bantock House Museum and Bilston Art Gallery and Museum (see chapter 7).

The centre of Wolverhampton is dominated by the imposing St Peter's church, which dates from the thirteenth century. A translation of Lady Wulfruna's charter of 985 hangs in the vestry, while in the gardens is the shaft of a Saxon pillar, the oldest man-made object in Wolverhampton.

St John's church is also of interest, dating from 1760 and built of brick with an outer

St Peter's church, Wolverhampton.

facing of stone. It possesses one of the most famous organs in England, an original Renatus Harris instrument of about 1633. Other historic buildings in the area include Moseley Old Hall and Wightwick Manor (see chapter 6).

Wolverhampton today is a busy and attractive town with shopping and entertainment facilities to contrast with the old. The Grand Theatre and Civic Hall attract artists of international repute and the town is the home of Banks's Park Brewery and the Springfield Brewery of Mitchells and Butlers.

WOMBOURNE

Wombourne dates from Saxon times but has grown dramatically since the 1950s as it lies within commuting distance of Wolverhampton and much of the Black Country. Buildings of interest include the Wodehouse, which dates from the thirteenth century, al-though the current buildings are part Jacobean and were restored in the nineteenth century. The house contains some attractive carvings, four-poster beds and an Elizabethan figure titled 'The Silent and Good Woman'. The church has a medieval tower and spire but was mostly rebuilt in the nineteenth century.

Wombourne stands beside the Staffordshire and Worcestershire Canal and there is a watermill and an intricate eighteenth-century lock, both of particular interest.

YOXALL

Yoxall is a small village on the edge of the once massive Needwood Forest. Most of the village is designated a conservation area, with many buildings of interest, including the parish church of St Peter. According to legend, Robin Hood was lord of the manor here and married Maid Marion at nearby Tutbury.

11
Tourist information centres

Burton upon Trent: Town Hall, King Edward Square. Telephone: 0283 45454.
Cannock: Prince of Wales Centre, Church Street. Telephone: 0543 578762.
Keele: M6 Service Area, Newcastle-under-Lyme. Telephone: 0782 712814.
Kinver: The Old House, 47 High Street. Telephone: 0384 872940.
Leek: Staffordshire Moorlands Information Centre, 1 Market Place, Leek. Telephone: 0538 399181 or 381000.
Lichfield: Donegal House, Bore Street. Telephone: 0543 252109.
Newcastle-under-Lyme: The Library, Ironmarket. Telephone: 0782 711964.
Stafford: Ancient High House, Greengate Street. Telephone: 0785 40204.
Stoke-on-Trent: Glebe Street, telephone: 0782 411222; Quadrant Road, Hanley, telephone: 0782 284600.
Tamworth: Council Offices, Marmion House, Lichfield Street. Telephone: 0827 311222.
Walsall: Walsall Central Library, Lichfield Street. Telephone: 0922 650067.
West Bromwich: Sandwell MBC Information Centre, Town Clerk's Department, Town Hall. Telephone: 021-569 2463.
Wolverhampton: 18 Queens Square. Telephone: 0902 321051.

STAFFORDSHIRE

* Country park, picnic area etc. (Ch.2)
∩ Archaeological site (Ch.3)
c Castle (Ch.4)
+ Church or other religious building (Ch.5)

▲ Historic building, garden (Ch.6)
M Museum, art gallery (Ch.7)
■ Town or village (Ch.8)
● Other places

Index

Page numbers in italics refer to illustrations.